Lectionary

Advent 2017 to the eve of Advent 2018 (Year B)

Church House Publishing

Published by Church House Publishing
Church House
Great Smith Street
London SW1P 3AZ

ISBN 978-0-7151-2328-7 (standard)
978-0-7151-2331-7 (large)

Authorization

The Common Worship Calendar and Lectionaries are authorized pursuant to Canon B 2 of the Canons of the Church of England for use until further resolution of the General Synod of the Church of England.

Edited by Peter Moger
Designed by Derek Birdsall & John Morgan/Omnific
Typeset by RefineCatch Ltd, Bungay, Suffolk
Printed in England by Core Publications Ltd

Contents of this booklet

This booklet gives details of the full range of possibilities envisaged in the liturgical calendar and lectionary of Common Worship. Its use as a tool for the preparation of worship will require the making of several choices based first on the general celebration of the Christian year by the Church of England as a whole; second on the customary pattern of calendar in the diocese, parish and place of worship; and third on the pattern of services locally.

The **first column** comprises the Calendar of the Church with the days of the year. Observances that are mandatory are printed either in **bold** type (Sundays), in **bold** type (Principal Feasts and Holy Days) or in roman (Festivals). Optional celebrations (Lesser Festivals) and Commemorations are printed in ordinary roman type and *italic* type respectively.

The **second column** comprises (a) the readings and psalms for the Principal Service on Sundays, Principal Feasts and Holy Days, and Festivals, and (b) Holy Communion readings and psalms for other days of the week. On the Sundays after Trinity, the Old Testament reading and its psalm are divided into two smaller columns, indicating a choice between a 'continuous' reading week by week or a reading 'related' to the Gospel for that day.

The **third column** comprises (a) the Third Service readings and psalms for Sundays, Principal Feasts and Holy Days, and Festivals, and (b) the readings and psalms for weekday Morning Prayer.

The **fourth column** comprises (a) the Second Service readings and psalms for Sundays, Principal Feasts and Holy Days, and Festivals, and (b) the readings and psalms for weekday Evening Prayer.

An **Additional Weekday Lectionary**, intended particularly for use in places of worship that attract occasional rather than daily worshippers, is provided on pages 72–79. It may be used at either Morning or Evening Prayer.

Common of the Saints

General readings and psalms for saints' days can be found on pages 81–85; for some particular celebrations, other readings are suggested there.

Special Occasions

Readings and psalms for special occasions can be found on pages 86–87.

Liturgical colours

Appropriate liturgical colours are suggested in this booklet. They are not mandatory; traditional or local use may be followed.

Colours are indicated by single letters: the first (always upper case) for the season or Festival; and occasionally a second (lower case) for an optional celebration on that day. Thus, for example, *Gr* for the celebration of a Lesser Festival whose liturgical colour is red, in an otherwise 'green' season.

The following abbreviations are used:

G	Green
P or p	Purple or Violet
P(La)	Purple or Lent array
R or r	Red
W or w	White (Gold is indicated where its use would be appropriate)

Notes on the Lectionary

Sundays, Principal Feasts and Holy Days and Festivals

Three sets of psalms and readings are provided for each Sunday, Principal Feast or Holy Day and Festival.

The **Principal Service lectionary** (based on the Revised Common Lectionary) is intended for use at the principal service of the day (whether this service is Holy Communion or some other authorized form). In most Church communities, this is likely to be the mid-morning service, but the minister is free to decide which service time normally constitutes the Principal Service of the day. This lectionary may be used twice if required – for example, at an early celebration of Holy Communion and then again at a later one.

If only **two readings** are used at the Principal Service and that service is Holy Communion, the second reading must always be the Gospel reading. When the Principal Service lectionary is used at a service other than Holy Communion, the Gospel reading need not always be chosen.

The **Second Service lectionary** is intended for a second main service. In many churches, this lectionary may be the appropriate provision for a Sunday afternoon or evening service. A Gospel reading is always provided so that this lectionary can, if necessary, be used where the second main service is a celebration of Holy Communion.

The **Third Service lectionary**, with shorter readings, is intended where a third set of psalms and readings is needed and is most appropriate for use at an office. A Gospel reading is not always provided, so this lectionary is not suitable for use at Holy Communion.

Weekdays

The Common Worship Weekday Lectionary authorized by the General Synod in 2005 comprises a lectionary (with psalms) for Holy Communion, a lectionary for Morning and Evening Prayer, and tables of psalms for Morning and Evening Prayer.

The **Daily Eucharistic Lectionary** (based on the Roman Catholic daily eucharistic lectionary) is a semi-continuous two-year lectionary with a wide use of scripture, though not complete coverage of the Bible. Two readings are provided for each day, the first from either the Old or New Testament, the second always a Gospel. Psalm provision is intended to be a brief response to the first reading. It is for use at Holy Communion normally in places with a daily or near-daily celebration with a regular congregation. It may also be used as an office lectionary.

The **lectionary for Morning and Evening Prayer** always provides two readings for each office, the first from the Old Testament and the second from the New Testament. These are generally in sequence. One of the New Testament readings for any particular day is from the Gospels.

The **psalms for Morning and Evening Prayer** follow a sequential pattern in Ordinary Time (apart from the period from All Saints to the beginning of Advent).

In the periods from All Saints until 18 December, from the Epiphany until the Presentation of Christ in the Temple (Candlemas), from Ash Wednesday until Palm Sunday, and from the Monday after Easter Week until Pentecost, there is a choice of psalms at Morning and Evening Prayer. The psalms printed first reflect the theme of the season. Alternatively, the psalms from the Ordinary Time cycle may be used. The two sets are separated by '*or*'.

From 19 December until the Epiphany and from the Monday of Holy Week until the Saturday of Easter Week, only seasonal psalms are provided.

Where more than one psalm is given, one psalm (printed in **bold**) may be used as the sole psalm at that office.

Guidance on how these options for saying the psalms are expressed typographically can be found in the 'Using the Lectionary tables' below.

A further cycle is provided (see table on page 88), which is largely the monthly sequential cycle of psalms given in the *Book of Common Prayer*.

A single psalm for use by those who only say one office each day is provided in Prayer During the Day in *Common Worship: Daily Prayer*.

An **Additional Weekday Lectionary**, intended particularly for use in places of worship that attract occasional rather than daily worshippers, is provided on pages 72–79. It can be used either at Morning or Evening Prayer. Psalmody is not provided and should be taken from provision outlined above.

Using the Lectionary tables

All **Bible references** (except to the Psalms) are to the *New Revised Standard Version* (New York, 1989). Those who use other Bible translations should check the verse numbers against the *NRSV*. Each reference gives book, chapter and verse, in that order.

References to the Psalms are to the Common Worship psalter, published in *Common Worship: Services and Prayers for the Church of England* (2000) and *Common Worship: Daily Prayer* (2005). A table showing the verse number differences between this and the psalter in the *Book of Common Prayer* is provided on the Common Worship website (http://www.churchofengland.org/prayer-worship/worship/texts/the-psalter/psalterverses.aspx).

Options in the provision of readings or psalms are presented in the following ways:

¶ square brackets [xx] give either optional additional verses or Psalms, or a shorter alternative;

¶ '*or*' indicates a simple choice between two alternative readings or courses of psalms;

¶ a psalm printed in **bold** may be used as the sole psalm at that office;

¶ on weekdays a psalm printed in parentheses (xx) is omitted if it has been used as the opening canticle at that office;

¶ a psalm marked with an asterisk may be shortened if desired.

Where a reading from the **Apocrypha** is offered, an alternative Old Testament reading is provided.

In the choice of **readings other than the Gospel** reading, the minister should ensure that, in any year, a balance is maintained between readings from the Old and New Testaments and that, where a particular biblical book is appointed to be read over several weeks, the choice ensures that the continuity of one book is not lost.

On the Sundays after Trinity, the Principal Service Lectionary provides **alternative Old Testament readings and psalms**. References in the left-hand column (under the heading 'Continuous') offer a *semi-continuous* reading of Old Testament texts. Such a reading and its complementary psalmody stand independently of the other readings. References in the right-hand column (under the heading 'Related') *relate* the Old Testament reading and the psalm to the Gospel reading. One column should be followed for the whole sequence of Sundays after Trinity.

The Lectionary 2017–2018

The Sunday and festal readings for 3 December 2017 (the First Sunday of Advent) to 1 December 2018 (the eve of Advent Sunday) are from **Year B**, which offers a semi-continuous reading of Mark's Gospel at the Principal Service on Sundays throughout the year.

The weekday readings for Holy Communion are from **Year Two** of the Daily Eucharistic Lectionary (DEL).

Office readings are from Table 1 of the Weekday Lectionary: at Morning Prayer, Old Testament 1 and New Testament 1; and, at Evening Prayer, Old Testament 2a and New Testament 2.

Notes on the Calendar 3 December 2017 — 1 December 2018

These notes are based on the Rules to Order the Christian Year (*Common Worship: Times and Seasons*, pages 24–30).

Sundays

All Sundays celebrate the paschal mystery of the death and resurrection of the Lord. They also reflect the character of the seasons in which they are set.

Principal Feasts

On these days (printed in **bold**) Holy Communion is celebrated in every cathedral and parish church, and this celebration, required by Canon B 14, may not be displaced by any other celebration, and may be dispensed with only in accordance with the provision of Canon B 14A.

Except in the case of Christmas Day and Easter Day, the celebration of the Feast *begins with Evening Prayer on the day before the Feast*, and the Collect at that Evening Prayer is that of the Feast. In the case of Christmas Eve and Easter Eve, there is proper liturgical provision (including a Collect) for the whole day.

The Epiphany may, for pastoral reasons, be celebrated on Sunday 7 January. **The Presentation of Christ in the Temple** (Candlemas) is celebrated on either Friday 2 February or Sunday 28 January. **All Saints' Day** may be celebrated on Sunday 4 November (replacing the Fourth Sunday before Advent), with or without a supplementary celebration on Thursday 1 November.

Other Principal Holy Days

These days (printed in **bold**), and the liturgical provision for them, may not be displaced by any other celebration.

Ash Wednesday (14 February) and **Maundy Thursday** (29 March) are Principal Holy Days. On both these days Holy Communion is celebrated in every cathedral or parish church, except where there is dispensation under Canon B 14A.

Good Friday (30 March) is a Principal Holy Day.

Eastertide

The paschal character of **the Great Fifty Days of Easter**, from Easter Day (1 April) to Pentecost (20 May), should be celebrated throughout the season, and should not be displaced by other celebrations. No Festival day may be celebrated in Easter Week; and nor may any Festival – except for a Patronal or Dedication Festival – displace the celebration of a Sunday (a memorial of the resurrection) during Eastertide. The paschal character of the season should be retained on those weekdays when saints' days are celebrated.

The three days before Ascension Day (7–9 May) are customarily observed as **Rogation Days**, when prayer is offered for God's blessing on the fruits of the earth and on human labour.

The nine days **after Ascension Day until the eve of Pentecost** (11–19 May) are observed as days of prayer and preparation for the celebration of the outpouring of the Holy Spirit.

Ordinary Time

Ordinary Time comprises two periods in the year: first, the period from the day after the Presentation of Christ in the Temple until the day before Ash Wednesday, and second, that from the day after Pentecost until the day before the First Sunday of Advent.

During Ordinary Time, there is no seasonal emphasis, except that the period between All Saints' Day and the First Sunday of Advent is a time to celebrate and reflect upon the reign of Christ in earth and heaven.

Festivals

These days (printed in roman), and the liturgical provision for them, are not usually displaced. For each day there is full liturgical provision for a Principal, Second and Third Service, and an optional so-called First Evening Prayer on the evening before the Festival where this is required.

Festivals may *not* be celebrated on Sundays in Advent, Lent or Eastertide, the Baptism of Christ, Ascension Day, Trinity Sunday or Christ the King, or weekdays between Palm Sunday and the Second Sunday of Easter.

Otherwise, Festivals falling on a Sunday – namely in 2017–18, the Birth of John the Baptist (falling on the Fourth Sunday after Trinity), Mary Magdalene (falling on the Eighth Sunday after Trinity) and Simon and Jude (falling on the Last Sunday after Trinity) – may be kept on that Sunday or transferred to the Monday (or, at the discretion of the minister, to the next suitable weekday).

Certain Festivals (namely, Thomas the Apostle, Matthias the Apostle, the Visit of the Blessed Virgin Mary to Elizabeth, and the Blessed Virgin Mary) have customary alternative dates (see page 8).

The Thursday after Trinity Sunday (31 May) may be observed as the **Day of Thanksgiving for the Institution of Holy Communion** (sometimes known as *Corpus Christi*), and may be kept as a Festival; if it is kept as a Festival, the Visit of the Blessed Virgin Mary to Elizabeth (if it is not kept on 2 July) is transferred to 1 June.

Other Celebrations

Mothering Sunday falls on the Fourth Sunday of Lent (11 March). Alternative prayers and readings are provided for the Principal Service. **Bible Sunday** may be celebrated on 28 October, replacing the Last Sunday after Trinity, and appropriate prayers and readings are provided.

Local Celebrations

The celebration of **the patron saint or the title of a church** is kept either as a Festival or as a Principal Feast.

The **Dedication Festival** of a church is the anniversary of the date of its dedication or consecration. This is kept either as a Festival or as a Principal Feast. When kept as Principal Feasts, the Patronal and Dedication Festivals may be transferred to the nearest Sunday, unless that day is already a Principal Feast or one of the following days: the First Sunday of Advent, the Baptism of Christ, the First Sunday of Lent, the Fifth Sunday of Lent, or Palm Sunday. If the actual date is not known, the Dedication Festival may be celebrated on 7 October (replacing the Nineteenth Sunday after Trinity), or on 28 October (replacing the Last Sunday after Trinity), or on a suitable date chosen locally. Readings can be found on page 80.

Harvest Thanksgiving may be celebrated on any Sunday in autumn, replacing the provision for that day, provided it does not displace any Principal Feast or Festival.

Diocesan and other local provision may be made in **the calendar of the saints** to supplement the general calendar, in accordance with Canon B 6, paragraph 5.

Lesser Festivals

Lesser Festivals (printed in ordinary roman type, in black) are observed in a manner appropriate to a particular place. Each is provided with a Collect, which may supersede the Collect of the week. For certain Lesser Festivals a complete set of Eucharistic readings is provided, and for others appropriate readings may be selected from the Common of the Saints (see pages 81–85). These readings may, at the minister's discretion, supersede the Daily Eucharistic Lectionary (DEL). The weekday psalms and readings at Morning and Evening Prayer are not usually superseded by those for Lesser Festivals, but at the minister's discretion psalms and readings provided on these days for use at Holy Communion may be used instead at Morning or Evening Prayer.

The minister may be selective in the Lesser Festivals that are observed and may also keep some, or all of them, as Commemorations, perhaps especially in Advent, Lent and Easter where the character of the season ought to be sustained. If the Day of Thanksgiving for the Institution of Holy Communion (31 May) is not kept as a Festival in 2018, it is not observed that year, and 31 May is kept as the Festival of the Visit of the Blessed Virgin Mary to Elizabeth.

When a Lesser Festival falls on a Principal Feast or Holy Day, a Festival, a Sunday, or on a weekday between Palm Sunday and the Second Sunday of Easter, its celebration is normally omitted for that year. However, where there is sufficient reason, it may, at the discretion of the minister, be celebrated on the nearest available day.

Commemorations

Commemorations (printed in *italic*) are made by a mention in prayers of intercession. They are not provided with Collect, Psalm and Readings, and do not replace the usual weekday provision at Holy Communion or at Morning and Evening Prayer.

The minister may be selective in the Commemorations that are made.

Only where there is an established celebration in the wider Church or where the day has a special local significance may a Commemoration be observed as a Lesser Festival, with liturgical provision from the Common of the Saints (pages 81–85).

In designating a Commemoration as a Lesser Festival, the minister must remember the need to maintain the spirit of the season, especially of Advent, Lent and Easter.

Days of Discipline and Self-Denial

The weekdays of Lent and every Friday in the year are days of discipline and self-denial, with the exception of Principal Feasts, Festivals outside Lent, and Fridays from Easter Day to Pentecost. The day preceding a Principal Feast may also be appropriately kept as a day of discipline and self-denial in preparation for the Feast.

Ember Days

Ember Days should be kept, under the bishop's directions, in the week before an ordination as days of prayer for those to be ordained deacon or priest.

Ember Days may also be kept even when there is no ordination in the diocese as more general days of prayer for those who serve the Church in its various ministries, both ordained and lay, and for vocations. Traditionally they have been observed on the Wednesday, Friday and Saturday in the week before the Third Sunday of Advent, the Second Sunday of Lent, and the Sundays nearest to 29 June and 29 September.

Notes on Collects

For a table showing where the Collects and Post Communions are published, see page 80.

Where a Collect ends 'through Jesus Christ . . . now and for ever', the minister may omit the longer (trinitarian) ending and use the shorter ending, 'through Jesus Christ our Lord', to which the people respond, 'Amen'. The longer ending, however, is to be preferred at a service of Holy Communion.

The Collect for each Sunday is used at Evening Prayer on the Saturday preceding, except where that Saturday is a Principal Feast, or a Festival, or the eve of Christmas Day or Easter Day. The Collect for each Sunday is also used on the weekdays following, except where other provision is made.

Abbreviations used in this book

Alt	Alternative
Bp	Bishop
BVM	Blessed Virgin Mary
DEL	Daily Eucharistic Lectionary
EP	Evening Prayer
G	Green
HC	Holy Communion: *used where additional references are given to provide alternative texts for use at a celebration of Holy Communion (most often the provision of a psalm or gospel)*
MP	Morning Prayer
P or p	Purple or Violet
P(La)	Purple or Lent Array
Ps & Pss	Psalmody
R or r	Red
W or w	White (Gold is indicated where its use would be appropriate)

Standard abbreviations have been used for other books of the Bible where necessary.

Alternative dates

The following may be celebrated on the alternative dates indicated:

Thomas the Apostle
– on 21 December 2017 instead of 3 July 2018
Matthias the Apostle
– on 24 February instead of 14 May
The Visit of the Blessed Virgin Mary to Elizabeth
– on 2 July instead of 31 May (or instead of 1 June, if Corpus Christi is kept as a Festival)
Thomas Becket
– on 7 July instead of 29 December 2017
Cuthbert
– on 4 September instead of 20 March
The Blessed Virgin Mary
– on 8 September instead of 15 August
Chad
– with Cedd on 26 October instead of 2 March

If any of the four festivals is celebrated on the alternative date these provisions should be used on the principal date:

Holy Communion	Morning Prayer	Evening Prayer
If Thomas the Apostle *is celebrated on Thursday 21 December 2017 the following provision is used on Tuesday 3 July 2018 (G):*		
Amos 3.1–8, 4.11–12	Psalm **106*** (*or* 103)	Psalm **107***
Psalm 5.8–end	1 Samuel 1.21—2.11	Nehemiah 13.1–14
If Matthias the Apostle *is celebrated on Saturday 24 February the following provision is used on Monday 14 May (W):*		
Acts 19.1–8	Psalms **93**, 96, 97 *or* **98**, 99, 101	Psalm **18** *or* **105*** (*or* 103)
Psalm 68.1–6	Numbers 22.1–35	Deuteronomy 31.1–13
John 16.29–end	Luke 7.36–end	1 John 2.18–end
	**Numbers 27.15–end; 1 Corinthians 3*	
If The Visit of the Blessed Virgin Mary to Elizabeth *is celebrated on Monday 2 July and* Corpus Christi *is not kept as a Festival, the following provision is used on Thursday 31 May (G):*		
1 Peter 2.2–5, 9–12	Psalms 14, **15**, 16	Psalm **18***
Psalm 100	Joshua 8.30–end	2 Chronicles 29.20–end
Mark 10.46–end	Luke 11.14–28	Romans 5.12–end
Or, if Corpus Christi *is kept as a Festival, the following provision is used on Thursday 31 May (W):*		
Genesis 14.18–20	*MP* Psalm 147	*EP* Psalms 23, 42, 43
Psalm 116.10–end	Deuteronomy 8.2–16	Proverbs 9.1–5
1 Corinthians 11.23–26	1 Corinthians 10.1–17	Luke 9.11–17
John 6.51–58		
Matthew 8.23–27	Luke 19.41–end	2 Corinthians 1.15—2.4
If The Blessed Virgin Mary *is celebrated on Saturday 8 September the following provision is used on Wednesday 15 August (G):*		
Ezekiel 9.1–7, 10.18–22	Psalm **119.105–128**	Psalms **91**, 93
Psalm 113	2 Samuel 6.1–19	Micah 3
Matthew 18.15–20	Acts 7.17–43	Mark 5.35–end

Key to the Tables

For guidance on how the options for saying the psalms are expressed typographically, see page 5.

Sundays (and Principal Feasts, other Principal Holy Days, and Festivals)

Day	Date	Colour	Principal Service	3rd Service	2nd Service
Day	**Date** Sunday / **Feast** † / Festival ††	*Colour*	Main service of the day: Holy Communion, Morning Prayer, Evening Prayer, or a Service of the Word	Shorter Readings, an Office lectionary probably used at Morning Prayer where Holy Communion is the Principal Service	2nd main Service, probably used at Evening Prayer; adaptable for Holy Communion

† Principal Feasts and other Principal Holy Days are printed in **bold**.
†† Festivals are printed in roman typeface.

Weekdays

Day	Date	Colour	Holy Communion	Morning Prayer	Evening Prayer
Day	**Date**	*Colour*	Weekday readings	Psalms and readings for Morning Prayer	Psalms and readings for Evening Prayer

Lesser Festival ‡* [optional]
Commemoration ‡‡ [optional]

‡ Lesser Festivals are printed in roman typeface, in black.
‡‡ Commemorations are printed in italics.
* The ascriptions given to holy men and women in the Calendar (such as martyr, teacher of the faith, etc.) have often been abbreviated in this booklet for reasons of space. The particular ascription given is there to be helpful if needing to choose Collects and readings from Common of the Saints; where several ascriptions are used (e.g. bishop and martyr), traditionally the last ascription given is the most important and therefore the guiding one. The full ascriptions may be found in the Calendar, which is printed in *Common Worship: Times and Seasons* (pages 7–22), *Common Worship: Festivals* (pages 5–20) and *Common Worship: Daily Prayer* (pages 5–16). These incorporate minor corrections made since the publication of the Calendar in *Common Worship: Services and Prayers for the Church of England* (pages 5–16).

		Principal Service	3rd Service	2nd Service
Sunday	**3 December** *P* **1st Sunday of Advent**	Isaiah 64.1–9 Psalm 80.1–8, 18–20 [*or* 80.1–8] 1 Corinthians 1.3–9 Mark 13.24–end	Psalm 44 Isaiah 2.1–5 Luke 12.35–48	Psalm 25 [*or* 25.1–9] Isaiah 1.1–20 Matthew 21.1–13
		Holy Communion	**Morning Prayer**	**Evening Prayer**
Monday	**4 December** *P* *John of Damascus, monk, teacher of the faith, c.749* *Nicholas Ferrar, deacon, founder of the Little Gidding Community, 1637*	Isaiah 2.1–5 Psalm 122 Matthew 8.5–11	Psalms **50**, 54 *or* **1**, 2, 3 Isaiah 25.1–9 Matthew 12.1–21	Psalms 70, **71** *or* **4**, 7 Isaiah 42.18–end Revelation 19
Tuesday	**5 December** *P*	Isaiah 11.1–10 Psalm 72.1–4, 18–19 Luke 10.21–24	Psalms **80**, 82 *or* **5**, 6 (8) Isaiah 26.1–13 Matthew 12.22–37	Psalms **74**, 75 *or* **9**, 10* Isaiah 43.1–13 Revelation 20
Wednesday	**6 December** *Pw* Nicholas, bishop, c.326 (see p.83)	Isaiah 25.6–10*a* Psalm 23 Matthew 15.29–37	Psalms 5, **7** *or* **119.1–32** Isaiah 28.1–13 Matthew 12.38–end	Psalms 76, **77** *or* **11**, 12, 13 Isaiah 43.14–end Revelation 21.1–8
Thursday	**7 December** *Pw* Ambrose, bishop, teacher of the faith, 397 (see p.82)	Isaiah 26.1–6 Psalm 118.18–27*a* Matthew 7.21, 24–27	Psalms **42**, 43 *or* 14, **15**, 16 Isaiah 28.14–end Matthew 13.1–23	Psalms **40**, 46 *or* **18*** Isaiah 44.1–8 Revelation 21.9–21
Friday	**8 December** *Pw* Conception of the Blessed Virgin Mary (see p.81)	Isaiah 29.17–end Psalm 27.1–4, 16–17 Matthew 9.27–31	Psalms **25**, 26 *or* 17, **19** Isaiah 29.1–14 Matthew 13.24–43	Psalms 16, **17** *or* **22** Isaiah 44.9–23 Revelation 21.22—22.5
Saturday	**9 December** *P*	Isaiah 30.19–21, 23–26 Psalm 146.4–9 Matthew 9.35—10.1, 6–8	Psalms **9** (10) *or* 20, 21, **23** Isaiah 29.15–end Matthew 13.44–end	Psalms **27**, 28 *or* **24**, 25 Isaiah 44.24—45.13 Revelation 22.6–end

		Principal Service	3rd Service	2nd Service
Sunday	**10 December** *P* **2nd Sunday of Advent**	Isaiah 40.1–11 Psalm 85.1–2, 8–end [*or* 85.8–end] 2 Peter 3.8–15*a* Mark 1.1–8	Psalm 80 Baruch 5.1–9 *or* Zephaniah 3.14–end Luke 1.5–20	Psalm 40 [*or* 40.12–end] 1 Kings 22.1–28 Romans 15.4–13 *HC* Matthew 11.2–11
		Holy Communion	**Morning Prayer**	**Evening Prayer**
Monday	**11 December** *P*	Isaiah 35 Psalm 85.7–end Luke 5.17–26	Psalm **44** *or* 27, **30** Isaiah 30.1–18 Matthew 14.1–12	Psalms **144**, 146 *or* 26, **28**, 29 Isaiah 45.14–end 1 Thessalonians 1
Tuesday	**12 December** *P*	Isaiah 40.1–11 Psalm 96.1, 10–end Matthew 18.12–14	Psalms **56**, 57 *or* 32, **36** Isaiah 30.19–end Matthew 14.13–end	Psalms **11**, 12, 13 *or* **33** Isaiah 46 1 Thessalonians 2.1–12
Wednesday	**13 December** *Pr* Lucy, martyr, 304 (see p.81) *Samuel Johnson, moralist, 1784* Ember Day	Isaiah 40.25–end Psalm 103.8–13 Matthew 11.28–end	Psalms **62**, 63 *or* **34** Isaiah 31 Matthew 15.1–20	Psalms **10**, 14 *or* **119.33–56** Isaiah 47 1 Thessalonians 2.13–end
Thursday	**14 December** *Pw* John of the Cross, poet, teacher of the faith, 1591 (see p.82)	Isaiah 41.13–20 Psalm 145.1, 8–13 Matthew 11.11–15	Psalms 53, **54**, 60 *or* **37*** Isaiah 32 Matthew 15.21–28	Psalm **73** *or* 39, **40** Isaiah 48.1–11 1 Thessalonians 3
Friday	**15 December** *P* Ember Day	Isaiah 48.17–19 Psalm 1 Matthew 11.16–19	Psalms 85, **86** *or* **31** Isaiah 33.1–22 Matthew 15.29–end	Psalms 82, **90** *or* **35** Isaiah 48.12–end 1 Thessalonians 4.1–12
Saturday	**16 December** *P* Ember Day	Ecclesiasticus 48.1–4, 9–11 *or* 2 Kings 2.9–12 Psalm 80.1–4, 18–19 Matthew 17.10–13	Psalm **145** *or* 41, **42**, 43 Isaiah 35 Matthew 16.1–12	Psalms 93, **94** *or* 45, **46** Isaiah 49.1–13 1 Thessalonians 4.13–end

Day	Date		Principal Service	3rd Service	2nd Service
Sunday	**17 December** **3rd Sunday of Advent** *O Sapientia*	*P*	Isaiah 61.1–4, 8–end Psalm 126 *or Canticle*: Magnificat 1 Thessalonians 5.16–24 John 1.6–8, 19–28	Psalms 50.1–6, 62 Isaiah 12 Luke 1.57–66	Psalm 68.1–19 [*or* 68.1–8] Malachi 3.1–4; 4 Philippians 4.4–7 *HC* Matthew 14.1–12
			Holy Communion	**Morning Prayer**	**Evening Prayer**
Monday	**18 December**	*P*	Jeremiah 23.5–8 Psalm 72.1–2, 12–13, 18–end Matthew 1.18–24	Psalm **40** *or* **44** Isaiah 38.1–8, 21–22 Matthew 16.13–end	Psalms 25, **26** *or* **47**, 49 Isaiah 49.14–25 1 Thessalonians 5.1–11
				From Tuesday 19 December until the Epiphany the seasonal psalmody must be used at Morning and Evening Prayer	
Tuesday	**19 December**	*P*	Judges 13.2–7, 24–end Psalm 71.3–8 Luke 1.5–25	Psalms 144, **146** Isaiah 38. 9–20 Matthew 17.1–13	Psalms 10, **57** Isaiah 50 1 Thessalonians 5.12–end
Wednesday	**20 December**	*P*	Isaiah 7.10–14 Psalm 24.1–6 Luke 1.26–38	Psalms **46**, 95 Isaiah 39 Matthew 17.14–21	Psalms **4**, 9 Isaiah 51.1–8 2 Thessalonians 1
Thursday	**21 December**	*P*	Zephaniah 3.14–18 Psalm 33.1–4, 11–12, 20–end Luke 1.39–45	Psalms **121**, 122, 123 Zephaniah 1.1—2.3 Matthew 17.22–end	Psalms 80, **84** Isaiah 51.9–16 2 Thessalonians 2
Friday	**22 December**	*P*	1 Samuel 1.24–end Psalm 113 Luke 1.46–56	Psalms **124**, 125, 126, 127 Zephaniah 3.1–13 Matthew 18.1–20	Psalms 24, **48** Isaiah 51.17–end 2 Thessalonians 3
Saturday	**23 December**	*P*	Malachi 3.1–4, 4.5–end Psalm 25.3–9 Luke 1.57–66	Psalms 128, 129, **130**, 131 Zephaniah 3.14–end Matthew 18.21–end	Psalm **89.1–37** Isaiah 52.1–12 Jude

Day	Date	Colour	Principal Service	3rd Service	2nd Service
Sunday	**24 December** **4th Sunday of Advent** **Christmas Eve**	*P*	2 Samuel 7.1–11,16 *Canticle*: Magnificat *or* Psalm 89.1–4, 19–26 [*or* 89.1–8] Romans 16.25–end Luke 1.26–38	Psalm 144 Isaiah 7.10–16 Romans 1.1–7	**EP of Christmas Eve** Psalm 85 Zechariah 2 Revelation 1.1–8
Monday	**25 December** Christmas Day	*Gold or W*	*Any of the following three sets of Principal Service readings may be used on the evening of Christmas Eve and on Christmas Day. Set III should be used at some service during the celebration.* **Set I**: Isaiah 9.2–7; Psalm 96; Titus 2.11–14; Luke 2.1–14 [15–20] **Set II**: Isaiah 62.6–end; Psalm 97; Titus 3.4–7; Luke 2. [1–7] 8–20 **Set III**: Isaiah 52.7–10; Psalm 98; Hebrews 1.1–4 [5–12]; John 1.1–14	*MP* Psalms **110**, 117 Isaiah 62.1–5 Matthew 1.18–end	*EP* Psalm 8 Isaiah 65.17–25 Philippians 2.5–11 *or* Luke 2.1–20 *if it has not been used at the principal service of the day*
Tuesday	**26 December** Stephen, deacon, first martyr	*R*	2 Chronicles 24.20–22 *or* Acts 7.51–end Psalm 119.161–168 Acts 7.51–end *or* Galatians 2.16*b*–20 Matthew 10.17–22	*MP* Psalms **13**, 31.1–8, 150 Jeremiah 26.12–15 Acts 6	*EP* Psalms 57, **86** Genesis 4.1–10 Matthew 23.34–end
Wednesday	**27 December** John, Apostle and Evangelist	*W*	Exodus 33.7–11*a* Psalm 117 1 John 1 John 21.19*b*–end	*MP* Psalms **21**, 147.13–end Exodus 33.12–end 1 John 2.1–11	*EP* Psalm **97** Isaiah 6.1–8 1 John 5.1–12
Thursday	**28 December** The Holy Innocents	*R*	Jeremiah 31.15–17 Psalm 124 1 Corinthians 1.26–29 Matthew 2.13–18	*MP* Psalms **36**, 146 Baruch 4.21–27 *or* Genesis 37.13–20 Matthew 18.1–10	*EP* Psalms 123, **128** Isaiah 49.14–25 Mark 10.13–16
			Holy Communion	**Morning Prayer**	**Evening Prayer**
Friday	**29 December** Thomas Becket, archbishop, martyr, 1170 (see p.81)	*Wr*	1 John 2.3–11 Psalm 96.1–4 Luke 2.22–35	Psalms **19**, 20 Jonah 1 Colossians 1.1–14	Psalms 131, **132** Isaiah 57.15–end John 1.1–18
Saturday	**30 December**	*W*	1 John 2.12–17 Psalm 96.7–10 Luke 2.36–40	Psalms 111, 112, **113** Jonah 2 Colossians 1.15–23	Psalms **65**, 84 Isaiah 59.1–15*a* John 1.19–28

		Principal Service	3rd Service	2nd Service
Sunday	**31 December** *W* **1st Sunday of Christmas**	Isaiah 61.10—62.3 Psalm 148 [*or* 148.7–end] Galatians 4.4–7 Luke 2.15–21	Psalm 105.1–11 Isaiah 63.7–9 Ephesians 3.5–12	Psalm 132 Isaiah 35 Colossians 1.9–20 *or* Luke 2.41–end *or:* 1st EP of the Naming and Circumcision of Jesus: Psalm 148 Jeremiah 23.1–6 Colossians 2.8–15
Monday	**1 January** *W* Naming and Circumcision of Jesus	Numbers 6.22–end Psalm 8 Galatians 4.4–7 Luke 2.15–21	*MP* Psalms **103**, 150 Genesis 17.1–13 Romans 2.17–end	*EP* Psalm **115** Deuteronomy 30. [1–10] 11–end Acts 3.1–16
		Holy Communion	**Morning Prayer**	**Evening Prayer**
Tuesday	**2 January** *W* Basil the Great and Gregory of Nazianzus, bishops, teachers of the faith, 379 and 389 (see p.82) *Seraphim, monk, spiritual guide, 1833* *Vedanayagam Samuel Azariah, bishop, evangelist, 1945*	1 John 2.22–28 Psalm 98.1–4 John 1.19–28	Psalm **18.1–30** Ruth 1 Colossians 2.8–end	Psalms 45, **46** Isaiah 60.1–12 John 1.35–42

If the Epiphany is celebrated on Saturday 6 January and the Baptism of Christ is celebrated on Sunday 7 January:

			Holy Communion	Morning Prayer	Evening Prayer
Wednesday	**3 January**	*W*	1 John 2.29—3.6 Psalm 98.2–7 John 1.29–34	Psalms **127**, 128, 131 Ruth 2 Colossians 3.1–11	Psalms **2**, 110 Isaiah 60.13–end John 1.43–end
Thursday	**4 January**	*W*	1 John 3.7–10 Psalm 98.1, 8–end John 1.35–42	Psalm **89.1–37** Ruth 3 Colossians 3.12—4.1	Psalms 85, **87** Isaiah 61 John 2.1–12
Friday	**5 January**	*W*	1 John 3.11–21 Psalm 100 John 1.43–end	Psalms 8, **48** Ruth 4.1–17 Colossians 4.2–end	**1st EP of the Epiphany:** Psalms 96, **97** Isaiah 49.1–13 John 4.7–26
			Principal Service	3rd Service	2nd Service
Saturday	**6 January** **Epiphany**	*Gold or W*	Isaiah 60.1–6 Psalm 72. [1–9] 10–15 Ephesians 3.1–12 Matthew 2.1–12	*MP* Psalms **132**, 113 Jeremiah 31.7–14 John 1.29–34	*EP* Psalms **98**, 100 Baruch 4.36—end of 5 *or* Isaiah 60.1–9 John 2.1–11
Sunday	**7 January** Baptism of Christ *1st Sunday of Epiphany*	*Gold or W*	Genesis 1.1–5 Psalm 29 Acts 19.1–7 Mark 1.4–11	Psalm 89.19–29 1 Samuel 16.1–3, 13 John 1.29–34	Psalms 46, 47 Isaiah 42.1–9 Ephesians 2.1–10 *HC* Matthew 3.13–end
			Holy Communion	Morning Prayer	Evening Prayer
Monday	**8 January** DEL week 1	*W*	1 Samuel 1.1–8 Psalm 116.10–15 Mark 1.14–20	Psalms **2**, 110 *or* **71** Genesis 1.1–19 Matthew 21.1–17	Psalms **34**, 36 *or* **72**, 75 Amos 1 1 Corinthians 1.1–17

Epiphany / Baptism of Christ

If the Epiphany is celebrated on Sunday 7 January and the Baptism of Christ is transferred to Monday 8 January:

			Holy Communion	Morning Prayer	Evening Prayer
Wednesday	**3 January**	*W*	1 John 2.29—3.6 Psalm 98.2–7 John 1.29–34	Psalms **127**, 128, 131 Ruth 2 Colossians 3.1–11	Psalms **2**, 110 Isaiah 60.13–end John 1.43–end
Thursday	**4 January**	*W*	1 John 3.7–10 Psalm 98.1, 8–end John 1.35–42	Psalm **89.1–37** Ruth 3 Colossians 3.12—4.1	Psalms 85, **87** Isaiah 61 John 2.1–12
Friday	**5 January**	*W*	1 John 3.11–21 Psalm 100 John 1.43–end	Psalms 8, **48** Ruth 4.1–17 Colossians 4.2–end	Psalms 96, **97** Isaiah 62 John 2.13–end
Saturday	**6 January**	*W*	1 John 5.5–13 Psalm 147.13–end Mark 1.7–11	Psalms **99**, 147.1–12 Baruch 1.15—2.10 *or* Jeremiah 23.1–8 Matthew 20.1–16	**1st EP of the Epiphany:** Psalms 96, **97** Isaiah 49.1–13 John 4.7–26
			Principal Service	**3rd Service**	**2nd Service**
Sunday	**7 January** **Epiphany**	*Gold or W*	Isaiah 60.1–6 Psalm 72. [1–9] 10–15 Ephesians 3.1–12 Matthew 2.1–12	*MP* Psalms **132**, 113 Jeremiah 31.7–14 John 1.29–34	*EP* Psalms **98**, 100 Baruch 4.36—end of 5 *or* Isaiah 60.1–9 John 2.1–11
Monday	**8 January** Baptism of Christ	*Gold or W*	Genesis 1.1–5 Psalm 29 Acts 19.1–7 Mark 1.4–11	Psalm 89.19–29 1 Samuel 16.1–3, 13 John 1.29–34	Psalms 46, 47 Isaiah 42.1–9 Ephesians 2.1–10 *HC* Matthew 3.13–end

		Holy Communion	Morning Prayer	Evening Prayer
Tuesday	**9 January** *W* DEL week 1	1 Samuel 1.9–20 *Canticle:* 1 Samuel 2.1, 4–8 *or* Magnificat Mark 1.21–28	Psalms 8, **9** *or* **73** Genesis 1.20—2.3 Matthew 21.18–32	Psalms **45**, 46 *or* **74** Amos 2 1 Corinthians 1.18–end
Wednesday	**10 January** *W* *William Laud, archbishop, 1645*	1 Samuel 3.1–10, 19–20 Psalm 40.1–4, 7–10 Mark 1.29–39	Psalms 19, **20** *or* **77** Genesis 2.4–end Matthew 21.33–end	Psalms **47**, 48 *or* **119.81–104** Amos 3 1 Corinthians 2
Thursday	**11 January** *W* *Mary Slessor, missionary, 1915*	1 Samuel 4.1–11 Psalm 44.10–15, 24–25 Mark 1.40–end	Psalms **21**, 24 *or* **78.1–39*** Genesis 3 Matthew 22.1–14	Psalms **61**, 65 *or* **78.40–end*** Amos 4 1 Corinthians 3
Friday	**12 January** *W* Aelred, abbot, 1167 (see p.84) *Benedict Biscop, scholar, 689*	1 Samuel 8.4–7, 10–end Psalm 89.15–18 Mark 2.1–12	Psalms **67**, 72 *or* **55** Genesis 4.1–16, 25–26 Matthew 22.15–33	Psalms **68** *or* **69** Amos 5.1–17 1 Corinthians 4
Saturday	**13 January** *W* Hilary, bishop, teacher of the faith, 367 (see p.82) *Kentigern (Mungo), missionary bishop, 603* *George Fox, founder of the Society of Friends (Quakers), 1691*	1 Samuel 9.1–4, 17–19, 10.1*a* Psalm 21.1–6 Mark 2.13–17	Psalms 29, **33** *or* **76**, 79 Genesis 6.1–10 Matthew 22.34–end	Psalms 84, **85** *or* 81, **84** Amos 5.18–end 1 Corinthians 5

			Principal Service	3rd Service	2nd Service
Sunday	**14 January** **2nd Sunday of Epiphany**	W	1 Samuel 3.1–10 [11–20] Psalm 139.1–5, 12–18 [*or* 139.1–9] Revelation 5.1–10 John 1.43–end	Psalm 145.1–12 Isaiah 62.1–5 1 Corinthians 6.11–end	Psalm 96 Isaiah 60.9–end Hebrews 6.17—7.10 *HC* Matthew 8.5–13
			Holy Communion	**Morning Prayer**	**Evening Prayer**
Monday	**15 January** DEL week 2	W	1 Samuel 15.16–23 Psalm 50.8–10, 16–17, 24 Mark 2.18–22	Psalms 145, **146** *or* **80**, 82 Genesis 6.11—7.10 Matthew 24.1–14	Psalm **71** *or* **85**, 86 Amos 6 1 Corinthians 6.1–11
Tuesday	**16 January**	W	1 Samuel 16.1–13 Psalm 89.19–27 Mark 2.23–end	Psalms **132**, 147.1–12 *or* 87, **89.1–18** Genesis 7.11–end Matthew 24.15–28	Psalm **89.1–37** *or* **89.19–end** Amos 7 1 Corinthians 6.12–end
Wednesday	**17 January** Antony of Egypt, hermit, abbot, 356 (see p.84) *Charles Gore, bishop, founder of the Community of the Resurrection, 1932*	W	1 Samuel 17.32–33, 37, 40–51 Psalm 144.1–2, 9–10 Mark 3.1–6	Psalms **81**, 147.13–end *or* **119.105–128** Genesis 8.1–14 Matthew 24.29–end	Psalms **97**, 98 *or* **91**, 93 Amos 8 1 Corinthians 7.1–24
Thursday	**18 January** **Week of Prayer for Christian Unity: 18–25 January** *Amy Carmichael, founder of the Dohnavur Fellowship, spiritual writer, 1951*	W	1 Samuel 18.6–9, 19.1–7 Psalm 56.1–2, 8–end Mark 3.7–12	Psalms **76**, 148 *or* 90, **92** Genesis 8.15—9.7 Matthew 25.1–13	Psalms 99, 100, **111** *or* **94** Amos 9 1 Corinthians 7.25–end
Friday	**19 January** Wulfstan, bishop, 1095 (see p.83)	W	1 Samuel 24.3–22*a* Psalm 57.1–2, 8–end Mark 3.13–19	Psalms **27**, 149 *or* **88** (95) Genesis 9.8–19 Matthew 25.14–30	Psalm **73** *or* **102** Hosea 1.1—2.1 1 Corinthians 8
Saturday	**20 January** *Richard Rolle, spiritual writer, 1349*	W	2 Samuel 1.1–4, 11–12, 17–19, 23–end Psalm 80.1–6 Mark 3.20–21	Psalms **122**, 128, 150 *or* 96, **97**, 100 Genesis 11.1–9 Matthew 25.31–end	Psalms **61**, 66 *or* **104** Hosea 2.2–17 1 Corinthians 9.1–14

		Principal Service	3rd Service	2nd Service
Sunday	**21 January** *W* **3rd Sunday of Epiphany**	Genesis 14.17–20 Psalm 128 Revelation 19.6–10 John 2.1–11	Psalm 113 Jonah 3.1–5,10 John 3.16–21	Psalm 33 [*or* 33.1–12] Jeremiah 3.21—4.2 Titus 2.1–8, 11–14 *HC* Matthew 4.12–23
		Holy Communion	**Morning Prayer**	**Evening Prayer**
Monday	**22 January** *W* *Vincent of Saragossa, deacon, martyr, 304* DEL week 3	2 Samuel 5.1–7, 10 Psalm 89.19–27 Mark 3.22–30	Psalms 40, **108** *or* **98**, 99, 101 Genesis 11.27—12.9 Matthew 26.1–16	Psalms **138**, 144 *or* **105*** (*or* 103) Hosea 2.18—end of 3 1 Corinthians 9.15–end
Tuesday	**23 January** *W*	2 Samuel 6.12–15, 17–19 Psalm 24.7–end Mark 3.31–end	Psalms 34, **36** *or* **106*** (*or* 103) Genesis 13.2–end Matthew 26.17–35	Psalm **145** *or* **107*** Hosea 4.1–16 1 Corinthians 10.1–13
Wednesday	**24 January** *W* Francis de Sales, bishop, teacher of the faith, 1622 (see p.82)	2 Samuel 7.4–17 Psalm 89.19–27 Mark 4.1–20	Psalms 45, **46** *or* 110, **111**, 112 Genesis 14 Matthew 26.36–46	Psalm 21, **29** *or* **119.129–152** Hosea 5.1–7 1 Corinthians 10.14—11.1 *or:* 1st EP of the Conversion of Paul Psalm 149 Isaiah 49.1–13 Acts 22.3–16
		Principal Service	**3rd Service**	**2nd Service**
Thursday	**25 January** *W* Conversion of Paul	Jeremiah 1.4–10 *or* Acts 9.1–22 Psalm 67 Acts 9.1–22 *or* Galatians 1.11–16*a* Matthew 19.27–end	*MP* Psalms 66, 147.13–end Ezekiel 3.22–end Philippians 3.1–14	*EP* Psalm 119.41–56 Ecclesiasticus 39.1–10 *or* Isaiah 56.1–8 Colossians 1.24—2.7
		Holy Communion	**Morning Prayer**	**Evening Prayer**
Friday	**26 January** *W* Timothy and Titus, companions of Paul	2 Samuel 11.1–10, 13–17 Psalm 51.1–6, 9 Mark 4.26–34 *Lesser Festival eucharistic lectionary:* Isaiah 61.1–3*a* Psalm 100 2 Timothy 2.1–8 *or* Titus 1.1–5 Luke 10.1–9	Psalms 61, **65** *or* **139** Genesis 16 Matthew 26.57–end	Psalms **67**, 77 *or* **130**, 131, 137 Hosea 6.7—7.2 1 Corinthians 11.17–end

Epiphany 4 / Presentation

If the Presentation of Christ is celebrated on Friday 2 February:

Day	Date	Colour	Holy Communion	Morning Prayer	Evening Prayer
Saturday	**27 January**	W	2 Samuel 12.1–7, 10–17 Psalm 51.11–16 Mark 4.35–end	Psalm **68** *or* 120, **121**, 122 Genesis 17.1–22 Matthew 27.1–10	Psalms **72**, 76 *or* **118** Hosea 8 1 Corinthians 12.1–11
			Principal Service	**3rd Service**	**2nd Service**
Sunday	**28 January** **4th Sunday of Epiphany**	W	Deuteronomy 18.15–20 Psalm 111 Revelation 12.1–5*a* Mark 1.21–28	Psalm 71.1–6, 15–17 Jeremiah 1.4–10 Mark 1.40–end	Psalm 34 [*or* 34.1–10] 1 Samuel 3.1–20 1 Corinthians 14.12–20 *HC* Matthew 13.10–17
			Holy Communion	**Morning Prayer**	**Evening Prayer**
Monday	**29 January** DEL week 4	W	2 Samuel 15.13–14, 30, 16.5–13 Psalm 3 Mark 5.1–20	Psalms **57**, 96 *or* 123, 124, 125, **126** Genesis 18.1–15 Matthew 27.11–26	Psalms 2, **20** *or* **127**, 128, 129 Hosea 9 1 Corinthians 12.12–end
Tuesday	**30 January** Charles, king and martyr, 1649 (see p.81)	*Wr*	2 Samuel 18.9–10, 14, 24–25, 30—19.3 Psalm 86.1–6 Mark 5.21–end	Psalms **93**, 97 *or* **132**, 133 Genesis 18.16–end Matthew 27.27–44	Psalms **19**, 21 *or* (134,) **135** Hosea 10 1 Corinthians 13
Wednesday	**31 January** *John Bosco, priest, founder of the Salesian Teaching Order, 1888*	W	2 Samuel 24.2, 9–17 Psalm 32.1–8 Mark 6.1–6*a*	Psalms **95**, 98 *or* **119.153–end** Genesis 19.1–3, 12–29 Matthew 27.45–56	Psalms **81**, 111 *or* **136** Hosea 11.1–11 1 Corinthians 14.1–19
Thursday	**1 February** *Brigid, abbess, c.525*	W	1 Kings 2.1–4, 10–12 *Canticle:* 1 Chronicles 29.10–12 *or* Psalm 145.1–5 Mark 6.7–13	Psalms 99, **110** *or* **143**, 146 Genesis 21.1–21 Matthew 27.57–end	**1st EP of the Presentation** Psalm 118 1 Samuel 1.19*b*–end Hebrews 4.11–end
			Principal Service	**3rd Service**	**2nd Service**
Friday	**2 February** **Presentation of Christ in the Temple** (Candlemas)	*Gold or W*	Malachi 3.1–5 Psalm 24. [1–6] 7–end Hebrews 2.14–end Luke 2.22–40	*MP* Psalms **48**, 146 Exodus 13.1–16 Romans 12.1–5	*EP* Psalms 122, **132** Haggai 2.1–9 John 2.18–22
			Holy Communion	**Morning Prayer**	**Evening Prayer**
Saturday	**3 February** Anskar, archbishop, missionary, 865 (see p.84)	*Gw*	1 Kings 3.4–13 Psalm 119.9–16 Mark 6.30–34	Psalm **147** Genesis 23 Matthew 28.16–end	Psalms **148**, 149, 150 Hosea 14 1 Corinthians 16.10–end

Ordinary Time begins today if the Presentation was celebrated on 2 February.
The Collect of 5 before Lent is used. DEL week 4

If the Presentation of Christ is transferred to Sunday 28 January:

Day	Date	Colour	Holy Communion	Morning Prayer	Evening Prayer
Saturday	**27 January**	*W*	2 Samuel 12.1–7, 10–17 Psalm 51.11–16 Mark 4.35–end	Psalm **68** *or* 120, **121**, 122 Genesis 17.1–22 Matthew 27.1–10	**1st EP of the Presentation:** Psalm 118 1 Samuel 1.19*b*–end Hebrews 4.11–end
			Principal Service	**3rd Service**	**2nd Service**
Sunday	**28 January** **Presentation of Christ in the Temple** (Candlemas)	*Gold or W*	Malachi 3.1–5 Psalm 24.[1–6] 7–end Hebrews 2.14–end Luke 2.22–40	*MP* Psalms **48**, 146 Exodus 13.1–16 Romans 12.1–5	*EP* Psalms 122, **132** Haggai 2.1–9 John 2.18–22
			Holy Communion	**Morning Prayer**	**Evening Prayer**
Monday	**29 January** Ordinary Time begins today if the Presentation was celebrated on 28 January The Collect of 5 before Lent is used DEL week 4	*G*	2 Samuel 15.13–14, 30, 16.5–13 Psalm 3 Mark 5.1–20	Psalms 123, 124, 125, **126** Genesis 18.1–15 Matthew 27.11–26	Psalms **127**, 128, 129 Hosea 9 1 Corinthians 12.12–end
Tuesday	**30 January** Charles, king and martyr, 1649 (see p.81)	*Gr*	2 Samuel 18.9–10, 14, 24–25, 30—19.3 Psalm 86.1–6 Mark 5.21–end	Psalms **132**, 133 Genesis 18.16–end Matthew 27.27–44	Psalms (134,) **135** Hosea 10 1 Corinthians 13
Wednesday	**31 January** *John Bosco, priest, founder of the Salesian Teaching Order, 1888*	*G*	2 Samuel 24.2, 9–17 Psalm 32.1–8 Mark 6.1–6*a*	Psalm **119.153–end** Genesis 19.1–3, 12–29 Matthew 27.45–56	Psalm **136** Hosea 11.1–11 1 Corinthians 14.1–19
Thursday	**1 February** *Brigid, abbess, c.525*	*G*	1 Kings 2.1–4, 10–12 *Canticle:* 1 Chronicles 29.10–12 *or* Psalm 145.1–5 Mark 6.7–13	Psalms **143**, 146 Genesis 21.1–21 Matthew 27.57–end	Psalms **138**, 140, 141 Hosea 11.12—end of 12 1 Corinthians 14.20–end
Friday	**2 February**	*G*	Ecclesiasticus 47.2–11 Psalm 18.31–36, 50–end Mark 6.14–29	Psalms 142, **144** Genesis 22.1–19 Matthew 28.1–15	Psalm **145** Hosea 13.1–14 1 Corinthians 16.1–9
Saturday	**3 February** Anskar, archbishop, missionary, 865 (see p.84)	*Gw*	1 Kings 3.4–13 Psalm 119.9–16 Mark 6.30–34	Psalm **147** Genesis 23 Matthew 28.16–end	Psalms **148**, 149, 150 Hosea 14 1 Corinthians 16.10–end

			Principal Service	3rd Service	2nd Service
Sunday	**4 February** **2nd Sunday before Lent**	*G*	Proverbs 8.1, 22–31 Psalm 104.26–end Colossians 1.15–20 John 1.1–14	Psalms 29, 67 Deuteronomy 8.1–10 Matthew 6.25–end	Psalm 65 Genesis 2.4*b*–end Luke 8.22–35
			Holy Communion	Morning Prayer	Evening Prayer
Monday	**5 February** DEL week 5	*G*	1 Kings 8.1–7, 9–13 Psalm 132.1–9 Mark 6.53–end	Psalms **1**, 2, 3 Genesis 29.31—30.24 2 Timothy 4.1–8	Psalms **4**, 7 2 Chronicles 9.1–12 John 19.1–16
Tuesday	**6 February** *Martyrs of Japan, 1597* *Accession of Queen Elizabeth II, 1952* (see p.87)	*G*	1 Kings 8.22–23, 27–30 Psalm 84.1–10 Mark 7.1–13	Psalms **5**, 6, (8) Genesis 31.1–24 2 Timothy 4.9–end	Psalms **9**, 10 2 Chronicles 10.1—11.4 John 19.17–30
Wednesday	**7 February**	*G*	1 Kings 10.1–10 Psalm 37.3–6, 30–32 Mark 7.14–23	Psalm **119.1–32** Genesis 31.25—32.2 Titus 1	Psalms **11**, 12, 13 2 Chronicles 12 John 19.31–end
Thursday	**8 February**	*G*	1 Kings 11.4–13 Psalm 106.3, 35–41 Mark 7.24–30	Psalms 14, **15**, 16 Genesis 32.3–30 Titus 2	Psalm **18*** 2 Chronicles 13.1—14.1 John 20.1–10
Friday	**9 February**	*G*	1 Kings 11.29–32; 12.19 Psalm 81.8–14 Mark 7.31–end	Psalms 17, **19** Genesis 33.1–17 Titus 3	Psalm **22** 2 Chronicles 14.2–end John 20.11–18
Saturday	**10 February** *Scholastica, abbess, c.543*	*G*	1 Kings 12.26–32; 13.33–end Psalm 106.6–7, 20–23 Mark 8.1–10	Psalms 20, 21, **23** Genesis 35 Philemon	Psalms **24**, 25 2 Chronicles 15.1–15 John 20.19–end

			Principal Service	3rd Service	2nd Service
Sunday	**11 February** **Sunday next before Lent**	*G*	2 Kings 2.1–12 Psalm 50.1–6 2 Corinthians 4.3–6 Mark 9.2–9	Psalms 27, 150 Exodus 24.12–end 2 Corinthians 3.12–end	Psalms 2, [99] 1 Kings 19.1–16 2 Peter 1.16–end *HC* Mark 9.[2–8] 9–13
			Holy Communion	**Morning Prayer**	**Evening Prayer**
Monday	**12 February** DEL week 6	*G*	James 1.1–11 Psalm 119.65–72 Mark 8.11–13	Psalms 27, **30** Genesis 37.1–11 Galatians 1	Psalms 26, **28**, 29 Jeremiah 1 John 3.1–21
Tuesday	**13 February**	*G*	James 1.12–18 Psalm 94.12–18 Mark 8.14–21	Psalms 32, **36** Genesis 37.12–end Galatians 2.1–10	Psalm **33** Jeremiah 2.1–13 John 3.22–end
			Principal Service	**3rd Service**	**2nd Service**
Wednesday	**14 February** Ash Wednesday	*P(La)*	Joel 2.1–2, 12–17 *or* Isaiah 58.1–12 Psalm 51.1–18 2 Corinthians 5.20*b*—6.10 Matthew 6.1–6, 16–21 *or* John 8.1–11	*MP* Psalm **38** Daniel 9.3–6, 17–19 1 Timothy 6.6–19	*EP* Psalm **51** *or* 102 [*or* 102.1–18] Isaiah 1.10–18 Luke 15.11–end
			Holy Communion	**Morning Prayer**	**Evening Prayer**
Thursday	**15 February** *Sigfrid, bishop, 1045* *Thomas Bray, priest, founder of SPCK and SPG, 1730*	*P(La)*	Deuteronomy 30.15–end Psalm 1 Luke 9.22–25	Psalm **77** *or* **37*** Genesis 39 Galatians 2.11–end	Psalm **74** *or* 39, **40** Jeremiah 2.14–32 John 4.1–26
Friday	**16 February**	*P(La)*	Isaiah 58.1–9*a* Psalm 51.1–5, 17–18 Matthew 9.14–15	Psalms **3**, 7 *or* **31** Genesis 40 Galatians 3.1–14	Psalm **31** *or* **35** Jeremiah 3.6–22 John 4.27–42
Saturday	**17 February** Janani Luwum, archbishop, martyr, 1977 (see p.81)	*P(La)r*	Isaiah 58.9*b*–end Psalm 86.1–7 Luke 5.27–32	Psalm **71** *or* 41, **42**, 43 Genesis 41.1–24 Galatians 3.15–22	Psalm **73** *or* 45, **46** Jeremiah 4.1–18 John 4.43–end

Day	Date		Principal Service	3rd Service	2nd Service
Sunday	**18 February** **1st Sunday of Lent**	*P(La)*	Genesis 9.8–17 Psalm 25.1–9 1 Peter 3.18–end Mark 1.9–15	Psalm 77 Exodus 34.1–10 Romans 10.8*b*–13	Psalm 119.17–32 Genesis 2.15–17; 3.1–7 Romans 5.12–19 *or* Luke 13.31–end
			Holy Communion	**Morning Prayer**	**Evening Prayer**
Monday	**19 February**	*P(La)*	Leviticus 19.1–2, 11–18 Psalm 19.7–end Matthew 25.31–end	Psalms 10, **11** *or* **44** Genesis 41.25–45 Galatians 3.23—4.7	Psalms 12, **13**, 14 *or* **47**, 49 Jeremiah 4.19–end John 5.1–18
Tuesday	**20 February**	*P(La)*	Isaiah 55.10–11 Psalm 34.4–6, 21–22 Matthew 6.7–15	Psalm **44** *or* **48**, 52 Genesis 41.46—42.5 Galatians 4.8–20	Psalms 46, **49** *or* **50** Jeremiah 5.1–19 John 5.19–29
Wednesday	**21 February** Ember Day	*P(La)*	Jonah 3 Psalm 51.1–5, 17–18 Luke 11.29–32	Psalms **6**, 17 *or* **119.57–80** Genesis 42.6–17 Galatians 4.21—5.1	Psalms 9, **28** *or* **59**, 60 (67) Jeremiah 5.20–end John 5.30–end
Thursday	**22 February**	*P(La)*	Esther 14.1–5, 12 –14 *or* Isaiah 55.6–9 Psalm 138 Matthew 7.7–12	Psalms **42**, 43 *or* 56, **57** (63*) Genesis 42.18–28 Galatians 5.2–15	Psalms 137, 138, **142** *or* 61, **62**, 64 Jeremiah 6.9–21 John 6.1–15
Friday	**23 February** Polycarp, bishop, martyr, c.155 (see p.81) Ember Day	*P(La)r*	Ezekiel 18.21–28 Psalm 130 Matthew 5.20–26	Psalm **22** *or* **51**, 54 Genesis 42.29–end Galatians 5.16–end	Psalms 54, **55** *or* **38** Jeremiah 6.22–end John 6.16–27
Saturday	**24 February** Ember Day	*P(La)*	Deuteronomy 26.16–end Psalm 119.1–8 Matthew 5.43–end	Psalms 59, **63** *or* **68** Genesis 43.1–15 Galatians 6	Psalms **4**, 16 *or* 65, **66** Jeremiah 7.1–20 John 6.27–40

Day	Date	Colour	Principal Service	3rd Service	2nd Service
Sunday	**25 February** **2nd Sunday of Lent**	*P(La)*	Genesis 17.1–7, 15–16 Psalm 22.23–end Romans 4.13–end Mark 8.31–end	Psalm 105.1–6, 37–end Isaiah 51.1–11 Galatians 3.1–9, 23–end	Psalm 135 [*or* 135.1–14] Genesis 12.1–9 Hebrews 11.1–3, 8–16 *HC* John 8.51–end
			Holy Communion	**Morning Prayer**	**Evening Prayer**
Monday	**26 February**	*P(La)*	Daniel 9.4–10 Psalm 79.8–9, 12, 14 Luke 6.36–38	Psalms 26, **32** *or* **71** Genesis 43.16–end Hebrews 1	Psalms 70, **74** *or* **72**, 75 Jeremiah 7.21–end John 6.41–51
Tuesday	**27 February** George Herbert, priest, poet, 1633 (see p.83)	*P(La)w*	Isaiah 1.10, 16–20 Psalm 50.8, 16–end Matthew 23.1–12	Psalm **50** *or* **73** Genesis 44.1–17 Hebrews 2.1–9	Psalms **52**, 53, 54 *or* **74** Jeremiah 8.1–15 John 6.52–59
Wednesday	**28 February**	*P(La)*	Jeremiah 18.18–20 Psalm 31.4–5, 14–18 Matthew 20.17–28	Psalm **35** *or* **77** Genesis 44.18–end Hebrews 2.10–end	Psalms **3**, 51 *or* **119.81–104** Jeremiah 8.18—9.11 John 6.60–end
Thursday	**1 March** David, bishop, patron of Wales, c.601 (see p.83)	*P(La)w*	Jeremiah 17.5–10 Psalm 1 Luke 16.19–end	Psalm **34** *or* **78.1–39*** Genesis 45.1–15 Hebrews 3.1–6	Psalm **71** *or* **78.40–end*** Jeremiah 9.12–24 John 7.1–13
Friday	**2 March** Chad, bishop, missionary, 672 (see p.84)	*P(La)w*	Genesis 37.3–4, 12–13, 17–28 Psalm 105.16–22 Matthew 21.33–43, 45–46	Psalms 40, **41** *or* **55** Genesis 45.16–end Hebrews 3.7–end	Psalms **6**, 38 *or* **69** Jeremiah 10.1–16 John 7.14–24
Saturday	**3 March**	*P(La)*	Micah 7.14–15, 18–20 Psalm 103.1–4, 9–12 Luke 15.1–3, 11–end	Psalms 3, **25** *or* **76**, 79 Genesis 46.1–7, 28–end Hebrews 4.1–13	Psalms **23**, 27 *or* 81, **84** Jeremiah 10.17–24 John 7.25–36

			Principal Service	3rd Service	2nd Service
Sunday	**4 March** **3rd Sunday of Lent**	*P(La)*	Exodus 20.1–17 Psalm 19 [*or* 19.7–end] 1 Corinthians 1.18–25 John 2.13–22	Psalm 18.1–25 Jeremiah 38 Philippians 1.1–26	Psalms 11, 12 Exodus 5.1—6.1 Philippians 3.4*b*–14 *or* Matthew 10.16–22
			Holy Communion	**Morning Prayer**	**Evening Prayer**
	The following readings may replace those provided for Holy Communion on any day during the Third Week of Lent: Exodus 17.1–7; Psalm 95.1–2, 6–end; John 4.5–42				
Monday	**5 March**	*P(La)*	2 Kings 5.1–15 Psalms 42.1–2; 43.1–4 Luke 4.24–30	Psalms **5**, 7 *or* **80**, 82 Genesis 47.1–27 Hebrews 4.14—5.10	Psalms 11, **17** *or* **85**, 86 Jeremiah 11.1–17 John 7.37–52
Tuesday	**6 March**	*P(La)*	Song of the Three 2, 11–20 *or* Daniel 2.20–23 Psalm 25.3–10 Matthew 18.21–end	Psalms 6, **9** *or* 87, **89.1–18** Genesis 47.28—end of 48 Hebrews 5.11—6.12	Psalms 61, 62, **64** *or* **89.19–end** Jeremiah 11.18—12.6 John 7.53–8.11
Wednesday	**7 March** Perpetua, Felicity and companions, martyrs, 203 (see p.81)	*P(La)r*	Deuteronomy 4.1, 5–9 Psalm 147.13–end Matthew 5.17–19	Psalm **38** *or* **119.105–128** Genesis 49.1–32 Hebrews 6.13–end	Psalms 36, **39** *or* **91**, 93 Jeremiah 13.1–11 John 8.12–30
Thursday	**8 March** Edward King, bishop, 1910 (see p.83) *Felix, bishop, 647* *Geoffrey Studdert Kennedy, priest, poet, 1929*	*P(La)w*	Jeremiah 7.23–28 Psalm 95.1–2, 6–end Luke 11.14–23	Psalms **56**, 57 *or* 90, **92** Genesis 49.33—end of 50 Hebrews 7.1–10	Psalms **59**, 60 *or* **94** Jeremiah 14 John 8.31–47
Friday	**9 March**	*P(La)*	Hosea 14 Psalm 81.6–10, 13, 16 Mark 12.28–34	Psalm **22** *or* **88** (95) Exodus 1.1–14 Hebrews 7.11–end	Psalm **69** *or* **102** Jeremiah 15.10–end John 8.48–end
Saturday	**10 March**	*P(La)*	Hosea 5.15—6.6 Psalm 51.1–2, 17–end Luke 18.9–14	Psalm **31** *or* 96, **97**, 100 Exodus 1.22—2.10 Hebrews 8	Psalms **116**, 130 *or* **104** Jeremiah 16.10—17.4 John 9.1–17

			Principal Service	3rd Service	2nd Service
Sunday	**11 March** **4th Sunday of Lent**	*P(La)*	Numbers 21.4–9 Psalm 107.1–3, 17–22 [*or* 107.1–9] Ephesians 2.1–10 John 3.14–21	Psalm 27 1 Samuel 16.1–13 John 9.1–25	Psalms 13, 14 Exodus 6.2–13 Romans 5.1–11 *HC* John 12.1–8

For Mothering Sunday:
Exodus 2.1–10 *or* 1 Samuel 1.20–end; Psalm 34.11–20 *or* 127.1–4;
2 Corinthians 1.3–7 *or* Colossians 3.12–17; Luke 2.33–35 *or* John 19.25*b*–27
If the Principal Service readings have been displaced by Mothering Sunday provisions, they may be used at the Second Service.

The following readings may replace those provided for Holy Communion on any day during the Fourth Week of Lent:
Micah 7.7–9; Psalm 27.1, 9–10, 16–17; John 9

			Holy Communion	Morning Prayer	Evening Prayer
Monday	**12 March**	*P(La)*	Isaiah 65.17–21 Psalm 30.1–5, 8, 11–end John 4.43–end	Psalms 70, **77** *or* **98**, 99, 101 Exodus 2.11–22 Hebrews 9.1–14	Psalms **25**, 28 *or* **105*** (*or* 103) Jeremiah 17.5–18 John 9.18–end
Tuesday	**13 March**	*P(La)*	Ezekiel 47.1–9, 12 Psalm 46.1–8 John 5.1–3, 5–16	Psalms 54, **79** *or* **106*** (*or* 103) Exodus 2.23—3.20 Hebrews 9.15–end	Psalms **80**, 82 *or* **107*** Jeremiah 18.1–12 John 10.1–10
Wednesday	**14 March**	*P(La)*	Isaiah 49.8–15 Psalm 145.8–18 John 5.17–30	Psalms 63, **90** *or* 110, **111**, 112 Exodus 4.1–23 Hebrews 10.1–18	Psalms 52, **91** *or* **119.129–152** Jeremiah 18.13–end John 10.11–21
Thursday	**15 March**	*P(La)*	Exodus 32.7–14 Psalm 106.19–23 John 5.31–end	Psalms 53, **86** *or* 113, **115** Exodus 4.27—6.1 Hebrews 10.19–25	Psalms **94** *or* 114, **116**, 117 Jeremiah 19.1–13 John 10.22–end
Friday	**16 March**	*P(La)*	Wisdom 2.1, 12–22 *or* Jeremiah 26.8–11 Psalm 34.15–end John 7.1–2, 10, 25–30	Psalm **102** *or* **139** Exodus 6.2–13 Hebrews 10.26–end	Psalms 13, **16** *or* **130**, 131, 137 Jeremiah 19.14—20.6 John 11.1–16
Saturday	**17 March** Patrick, bishop, missionary, patron of Ireland, c.460 (see p.84)	*P(La)w*	Jeremiah 11.18–20 Psalm 7.1–2, 8–10 John 7.40–52	Psalm **32** *or* 120, **121**, 122 Exodus 7.8–end Hebrews 11.1–16	Psalms **140**, 141, 142 *or* **118** Jeremiah 20.7–end John 11.17–27

Day	Date		Principal Service	3rd Service	2nd Service
Sunday	**18 March** **5th Sunday of Lent** *Passiontide begins*	*P(La)*	Jeremiah 31.31–34 Psalm 51.1–13 *or* Psalm 119.9–16 Hebrews 5.5–10 John 12.20–33	Psalm 107.1–22 Exodus 24.3–8 Hebrews 12.18–end	Psalm 34 [*or* 34.1–10] Exodus 7.8–24 Romans 5.12–end *HC* Luke 22.1–13 *or:* 1st EP of Joseph of Nazareth: Psalm 132 Hosea 11.1–9 Luke 2.41–end
Monday	**19 March** Joseph of Nazareth	*W*	2 Samuel 7.4–16 Psalm 89.26–36 Romans 4.13–18 Matthew 1.18–end	*MP* Psalms 25, 147.1–12 Isaiah 11.1–10 Matthew 13.54–end	*EP* Psalms 1, 112 Genesis 50.22–end Matthew 2.13–end
			Holy Communion	Morning Prayer	Evening Prayer
	The following readings may replace those provided for Holy Communion on any day during the Fifth Week of Lent: 2 Kings 4.18–21, 32–37; Psalm 17.1–8, 16; John 11.1–45				
Tuesday	**20 March** Cuthbert, bishop, missionary, 687 (see p.84)	*P(La)w*	Numbers 21.4–9 Psalm 102.1–3, 16–23 John 8.21–30	Psalms **35**, 123 *or* **132**, 133 Exodus 8.20–end Hebrews 11.32—12.2	Psalms **61**, 64 *or* (134,) **135** Jeremiah 22.1–5, 13–19 John 11.45–end
Wednesday	**21 March** Thomas Cranmer, archbishop, Reformation martyr, 1556 (see p.81)	*P(La)r*	Daniel 3.14–20, 24–25, 28 *Canticle*: Bless the Lord John 8.31–42	Psalms **55**, 124 *or* **119.153–end** Exodus 9.1–12 Hebrews 12.3–13	Psalms 56, **62** *or* **136** Jeremiah 22.20—23.8 John 12.1–11
Thursday	**22 March**	*P(La)*	Genesis 17.3–9 Psalm 105.4–9 John 8.51–end	Psalms **40**, 125 *or* **143**, 146 Exodus 9.13–end Hebrews 12.14–end	Psalms 42, **43** *or* **138**, 140, 141 Jeremiah 23.9–32 John 12.12–19
Friday	**23 March**	*P(La)*	Jeremiah 20.10–13 Psalm 18.1–6 John 10.31–end	Psalms **22**, 126 *or* 142, **144** Exodus 10 Hebrews 13.1–16	Psalm **31** *or* **145** Jeremiah 24 John 12.20–36*a*
Saturday	**24 March** *Walter Hilton, mystic, 1396* *Paul Couturier, priest, ecumenist, 1953* *Oscar Romero, archbishop, martyr, 1980*	*P(La)*	Ezekiel 37.21–end *Canticle*: Jeremiah 31.10–13 *or* Psalm 121 John 11.45–end	Psalms **23**, 127 *or* **147** Exodus 11 Hebrews 13.17–end	Psalms 118, 129, **130** *or* **148**, 149, 150 Jeremiah 25.1–14 John 12.36*b*–end

			Principal Service		3rd Service	2nd Service
Sunday	**25 March** **Palm Sunday**	*R*	*Liturgy of the Palms:* Mark 11.1–11 *or* John 12.12–16 Psalm 118.1–2,19–end [*or* 118.19–end]	*Liturgy of the Passion:* Isaiah 50.4–9*a* Psalm 31.9–16 [*or* 31.9–18] Philippians 2.5–11 Mark 14.1—end of 15 *or* Mark 15.1–39 [40–end]	Psalms 61, 62 Zechariah 9.9–12 1 Corinthians 2.1–12	Psalm 69.1–20 Isaiah 5.1–7 Mark 12.1–12

			Holy Communion	Morning Prayer	Evening Prayer
				From the Monday of Holy Week until the Saturday of Easter Week the seasonal psalmody must be used.	
Monday	**26 March** Monday of Holy Week	*R*	Isaiah 42.1–9 Psalm 36.5–11 Hebrews 9.11–15 John 12.1–11	Psalm 41 Lamentations 1.1–12*a* Luke 22.1–23	Psalm 25 Lamentations 2.8–19 Colossians 1.18–23
Tuesday	**27 March** Tuesday of Holy Week	*R*	Isaiah 49.1–7 Psalm 71.1–14 [*or* 71.1–8] 1 Corinthians 1.18–31 John 12.20–36	Psalm 27 Lamentations 3.1–18 Luke 22. [24–38] 39–53	Psalm 55.13–24 Lamentations 3.40–51 Galatians 6.11–end
Wednesday	**28 March** Wednesday of Holy Week	*R*	Isaiah 50.4–9*a* Psalm 70 Hebrews 12.1–3 John 13.21–32	Psalm 102 [*or* 102.1–18] Wisdom 1.16—2.1; 2.12–22 *or* Jeremiah 11.18–20 Luke 22.54–end	Psalm 88 Isaiah 63.1–9 Revelation 14.18—15.4
Thursday	**29 March** **Maundy Thursday**	*W*	Exodus 12.1–4 [5–10] 11–14 Psalm 116.1, 10–end [*or* 116.9–end] 1 Corinthians 11.23–26 John 13.1–17, 31*b*–35	Psalms 42, 43 Leviticus 16.2–24 Luke 23.1–25	Psalm 39 Exodus 11 Ephesians 2.11–18
Friday	**30 March** **Good Friday**	*Hangings removed; R for the Liturgy*	Isaiah 52.13—end of 53 Psalm 22 [*or* 22.1–11 *or* 22.1–21] Hebrews 10.16–25 *or* Hebrews 4.14–16; 5.7–9 John 18.1—end of 19	Psalm 69 Genesis 22.1–18 *A part of John 18 and 19 may be read, if not used at the Principal Service* *or* Hebrews 10.1–10	Psalms 130, 143 Lamentations 5.15–end John 19.38–end *or* Colossians 1.18–23

		Principal Service	3rd Service	2nd Service
Saturday	**31 March** *Hangings removed* **Easter Eve** *These readings are for use at services other than the Easter Vigil.*	Job 14.1–14 *or* Lamentations 3.1–9, 19–24 Psalm 31.1–4, 15–16 [*or* 31.1–5] 1 Peter 4.1–8 Matthew 27.57–end *or* John 19.38–end	Psalm 142 Hosea 6.1–6 John 2.18–22	Psalm 116 Job 19.21–27 1 John 5.5–12
		Vigil Readings	Complementary Psalmody	
Saturday *or* **Sunday**	**31 March evening** **1 April morning** *Gold or W* *Easter Vigil* *The New Testament readings should be preceded by a minimum of three Old Testament readings.* *The Exodus reading should always be used.*	Genesis 1.1—2.4*a* Genesis 7.1–5, 11–18; 8.6–18; 9.8–13 Genesis 22.1–18 **Exodus 14.10–end; 15.20–21** Isaiah 55.1–11 Baruch 3.9–15, 32—4.4 *or* Proverbs 8.1–8, 19–21; 9.4*b*–6 Ezekiel 36.24–28 Ezekiel 37.1–14 Zephaniah 3.14–end **Romans 6.3–11** **Mark 16.1–8**	Psalm 136.1–9, 23–end Psalm 46 Psalm 16 ***Canticle:* Exodus 15.1*b*–13, 17–18** *Canticle:* Isaiah 12.2–end Psalm 19 Psalms 42, 43 Psalm 143 Psalm 98 **Psalm 114**	
		Principal Service	3rd Service	2nd Service
Sunday	**1 April** *Gold or W* Easter Day	Acts 10.34–43 † *or* Isaiah 25.6–9 Psalm 118.1–2, 14–24 [*or* 118.14–24] 1 Corinthians 15.1–11 *or* Acts 10.34–43 † John 20.1–18 *or* Mark 16.1–8 † *The reading from Acts must be used as either the first or second reading.*	*MP* Psalms 114, 117 Genesis 1.1–5, 26–end 2 Corinthians 5.14—6.2	*EP* Psalms 105 *or* 66.1–11 Ezekiel 37.1–14 Luke 24.13–35

			Holy Communion	Morning Prayer	Evening Prayer
Monday	**2 April** Monday of Easter Week	W	Acts 2.14, 22–32 Psalm 16.1–2, 6–end Matthew 28.8–15	Psalms **111**, 117, 146 Exodus 12.1–14 1 Corinthians 15.1–11	Psalm **135** Song of Solomon 1.9—2.7 Mark 16.1–8
Tuesday	**3 April** Tuesday of Easter Week	W	Acts 2.36–41 Psalm 33.4–5, 18–end John 20.11–18	Psalms **112**, 147.1–12 Exodus 12.14–36 1 Corinthians 15.12–19	Psalm **136** Song of Solomon 2.8–end Luke 24.1–12
Wednesday	**4 April** Wednesday of Easter Week	W	Acts 3.1–10 Psalm 105.1–9 Luke 24.13–35	Psalms **113**, 147.13–end Exodus 12.37–end 1 Corinthians 15.20–28	Psalm **105** Song of Solomon 3 Matthew 28.16–end
Thursday	**5 April** Thursday of Easter Week	W	Acts 3.11–end Psalm 8 Luke 24.35–48	Psalms **114**, 148 Exodus 13.1–16 1 Corinthians 15.29–34	Psalm **106** Song of Solomon 5.2—6.3 Luke 7.11–17
Friday	**6 April** Friday of Easter Week	W	Acts 4.1–12 Psalm 118.1–4, 22–26 John 21.1–14	Psalms **115**, 149 Exodus 13.17—14.14 1 Corinthians 15.35–50	Psalm **107** Song of Solomon 7.10—8.4 Luke 8.41–end
Saturday	**7 April** Saturday of Easter Week	W	Acts 4.13–21 Psalm 118.1–4, 14–21 Mark 16.9–15	Psalms **116**, 150 Exodus 14.15–end 1 Corinthians 15.51–end	Psalm **145** Song of Solomon 8.5–7 John 11.17–44

			Principal Service	3rd Service	2nd Service
Sunday	**8 April** **2nd Sunday of Easter**	*W*	[Exodus 14.10–end; 15.20–21] Acts 4.32–35 † Psalm 133 1 John 1.1—2.2 John 20.19–end † *The reading from Acts must be used as either the first or second reading.*	Psalm 22.20–31 Isaiah 53.6–12 Romans 4.13–25	**1st EP of the Annunciation** Psalm 85 Wisdom 9.1–12 *or* Genesis 3.8–15 Galatians 4.1–5
Monday	**9 April** **Annunciation of Our Lord to the Blessed Virgin Mary** *(transferred from 25 March)*	*Gold or W*	Isaiah 7.10–14 Psalm 40.5–11 Hebrews 10.4–10 Luke 1.26–38	*MP* Psalms 111, 113 1 Samuel 2.1–10 Romans 5.12–end	*EP* Psalms 131, 146 Isaiah 52.1–12 Hebrews 2.5–end
			Holy Communion	**Morning Prayer**	**Evening Prayer**
Tuesday	**10 April** William Law, priest, spiritual writer, 1761 (see p.82) *William of Ockham, friar, philosopher, teacher of the faith, 1347*	*W*	Acts 4.32–end Psalm 93 John 3.7–15	Psalms **8**, 20, 21 *or* **5**, 6, (8) Exodus 15.22—16.10 Colossians 1.15–end	Psalm **104** *or* **9**, 10* Deuteronomy 1.19–40 John 20.11–18
Wednesday	**11 April** *George Selwyn, bishop, 1878*	*W*	Acts 5.17–26 Psalm 34.1–8 John 3.16–21	Psalms 16, **30** *or* **119.1–32** Exodus 16.11–end Colossians 2.1–15	Psalm **33** *or* **11**, 12, 13 Deuteronomy 3.18–end John 20.19–end
Thursday	**12 April**	*W*	Acts 5.27–33 Psalm 34.1, 15–end John 3.31–end	Psalms **28**, 29 *or* 14, **15**, 16 Exodus 17 Colossians 2.16—3.11	Psalm **34** *or* **18*** Deuteronomy 4.1–14 John 21.1–14
Friday	**13 April**	*W*	Acts 5.34–42 Psalm 27.1–5, 16–17 John 6.1–15	Psalms 57, **61** *or* 17, **19** Exodus 18.1–12 Colossians 3.12—4.1	Psalm **118** *or* **22** Deuteronomy 4.15–31 John 21.15–19
Saturday	**14 April**	*W*	Acts 6.1–7 Psalm 33.1–5, 18–19 John 6.16–21	Psalms 63, **84** *or* 20, 21, **23** Exodus 18.13–end Colossians 4.2–end	Psalm **66** *or* **24**, 25 Deuteronomy 4.32–40 John 21.20–end

			Principal Service	3rd Service	2nd Service
Sunday	**15 April** **3rd Sunday of Easter**	*W*	[Zephaniah 3.14–end] Acts 3.12–19 † Psalm 4 1 John 3.1–7 Luke 24.36*b*–48 *† The reading from Acts must be used as either the first or second reading.*	Psalm 77.11–20 Isaiah 63.7–15 1 Corinthians 10.1–13	Psalm 142 Deuteronomy 7.7–13 Revelation 2.1–11 *HC* Luke 16.19–end
			Holy Communion	Morning Prayer	Evening Prayer
Monday	**16 April** *Isabella Gilmore, deaconess, 1923*	*W*	Acts 6.8–15 Psalm 119.17–24 John 6.22–29	Psalms **96**, 97 *or* 27, **30** Exodus 19 Luke 1.1–25	Psalm **61**, 65 *or* 26, **28**, 29 Deuteronomy 5.1–22 Ephesians 1.1–14
Tuesday	**17 April**	*W*	Acts 7.51—8.1*a* Psalm 31.1–5, 16 John 6.30–35	Psalms **98**, 99, 100 *or* 32, **36** Exodus 20.1–21 Luke 1.26–38	Psalm **71** *or* **33** Deuteronomy 5.22–end Ephesians 1.15–end
Wednesday	**18 April**	*W*	Acts 8.1*b*–8 Psalm 66.1–6 John 6.35–40	Psalm **105** *or* **34** Exodus 24 Luke 1.39–56	Psalms 67, **72** *or* **119.33–56** Deuteronomy 6 Ephesians 2.1–10
Thursday	**19 April** Alphege, archbishop, martyr, 1012 (see p.81)	*Wr*	Acts 8.26–end Psalm 66.7–8, 14–end John 6.44–51	Psalm **136** *or* **37*** Exodus 25.1–22 Luke 1.57–end	Psalms **73** *or* 39, **40** Deuteronomy 7.1–11 Ephesians 2.11–end
Friday	**20 April**	*W*	Acts 9.1–20 Psalm 117 John 6.52–59	Psalm **107** *or* **31** Exodus 28.1–4*a*, 29–38 Luke 2.1–20	Psalm **77** *or* **35** Deuteronomy 7.12–end Ephesians 3.1–13
Saturday	**21 April** Anselm, abbot, archbishop, teacher of the faith, 1109 (see p.82)	*W*	Acts 9.31–42 Psalm 116.10–15 John 6.60–69	Psalms 108, **110**, 111 *or* 41, **42**, 43 Exodus 29.1–9 Luke 2.21–40	Psalms 23, **27** *or* 45, **46** Deuteronomy 8 Ephesians 3.14–end

Day	Date	Colour	Principal Service	3rd Service	2nd Service
Sunday	**22 April** **4th Sunday of Easter**	*W*	[Genesis 7.1–5, 11–18; 8.6–18; 9.8–13] Acts 4.5–12 † Psalm 23 1 John 3.16–end John 10.11–18 † *The reading from Acts must be used as either the first or second reading.*	Psalm 119.89–96 Nehemiah 7.73*b*—8.12 Luke 24.25–32	Psalm 81.8–16 Exodus 16.4–15 Revelation 2.12–17 *HC* John 6.30–40 *or:* 1st EP of George, martyr, patron of England: Psalms 111, 116 Jeremiah 15.15–end Hebrews 11.32—12.2
Monday	**23 April** George, martyr, patron of England, c.304	*R*	1 Maccabees 2.59–64 *or* Revelation 12.7–12 Psalm 126 2 Timothy 2.3–13 John 15.18–21	*MP* Psalms 5, 146 Joshua 1.1–9 Ephesians 6.10–20	*EP* Psalms 3, 11 Isaiah 43.1–7 John 15.1–8
			Holy Communion	**Morning Prayer**	**Evening Prayer**
Tuesday	**24 April** *Mellitus, bishop, 624* *Seven Martyrs of the Melanesian Brotherhood, 2003*	*W*	Acts 11.19–26 Psalm 87 John 10.22–30	Psalm **139** *or* **48**, 52 Exodus 32.15–34 Luke 3.1–14	Psalms 115, **116** *or* **50** Deuteronomy 9.23—10.5 Ephesians 4.17–end *or:* 1st EP of Mark the Evangelist: Psalm 19 Isaiah 52.7–10 Mark 1.1–15
			Principal Service	**3rd Service**	**2nd Service**
Wednesday	**25 April** Mark the Evangelist	*R*	Proverbs 15.28–end *or* Acts 15.35–end Psalm 119.9–16 Ephesians 4.7–16 Mark 13.5–13	*MP* Psalms 37.23–end, 148 Isaiah 62.6–10 *or* Ecclesiasticus 51.13–end Acts 12.25—13.13	*EP* Psalm 45 Ezekiel 1.4–14 2 Timothy 4.1–11
			Holy Communion	**Morning Prayer**	**Evening Prayer**
Thursday	**26 April**	*W*	Acts 13.13–25 Psalm 89.1–2, 20–26 John 13.16–20	Psalm **118** *or* 56, **57** (63*) Exodus 34.1–10, 27–end Luke 4.1–13	Psalms 81, **85** *or* 61, **62**, 64 Deuteronomy 11.8–end Ephesians 5.15–end
Friday	**27 April** *Christina Rossetti, poet, 1894*	*W*	Acts 13.26–33 Psalm 2 John 14.1–6	Psalm **33** *or* **51,** 54 Exodus 35.20—36.7 Luke 4.14–30	Psalms **36**, 40 *or* **38** Deuteronomy 12.1–14 Ephesians 6.1–9
Saturday	**28 April** *Peter Chanel, missionary, martyr, 1841*	*W*	Acts 13.44–end Psalm 98.1–5 John 14.7–14	Psalm **34** *or* **68** Exodus 40.17–end Luke 4.31–37	Psalms **84**, 86 *or* 65, **66** Deuteronomy 15.1–18 Ephesians 6.10–end

Day	Date	Colour			
			Principal Service	**3rd Service**	**2nd Service**
Sunday	**29 April** **5th Sunday of Easter**	*W*	[Baruch 3.9–15, 32—4.4 *or* Genesis 22.1–18] Acts 8.26–end † Psalm 22.25–end 1 John 4.7–end John 15.1–8 † *The reading from Acts must be used as either the first or second reading.*	Psalm 44.16–end 2 Maccabees 7.7–14 *or* Daniel 3.16–28 Hebrews 11.32—12.2	Psalm 96 Isaiah 60.1–14 Revelation 3.1–13 *HC* Mark 16.9–16
			Holy Communion	**Morning Prayer**	**Evening Prayer**
Monday	**30 April** *Pandita Mary Ramabai, translator, 1922*	*W*	Acts 14.5–18 Psalm 118.1–3, 14–15 John 14.21–26	Psalm **145** *or* **71** Numbers 9.15–end; 10.33–end Luke 4.38–end	Psalm **105** *or* **72**, 75 Deuteronomy 16.1–20 1 Peter 1.1–12 *or:* 1st EP of Philip and James, Apostles: Psalm 25; Isaiah 40.27–end; John 12.20–26
			Principal Service	**3rd Service**	**2nd Service**
Tuesday	**1 May** Philip and James, Apostles	*R*	Isaiah 30.15–21 Psalm 119.1–8 Ephesians 1.3–10 John 14.1–14	*MP* Psalms 139, 146 Proverbs 4.10–18 James 1.1–12	*EP* Psalm 149 Job 23.1–12 John 1.43–end
			Holy Communion	**Morning Prayer**	**Evening Prayer**
Wednesday	**2 May** Athanasius, bishop, teacher of the faith, 373 (see p.82)	*W*	Acts 15.1–6 Psalm 122.1–5 John 15.1–8	Psalms **30**, 147.13–end *or* **77** Numbers 12 Luke 5.12–26	Psalms 98, **99**, 100 *or* **119.81–104** Deuteronomy 18.9–end 1 Peter 2.1–10
Thursday	**3 May**	*W*	Acts 15.7–21 Psalm 96.1–3, 7–10 John 15.9–11	Psalms **57**, 148 *or* **78.1–39*** Numbers 13.1–3, 17–end Luke 5.27–end	Psalm **104** *or* **78.40–end*** Deuteronomy 19 1 Peter 2.11–end
Friday	**4 May** English saints and martyrs of the Reformation Era	*W*	Acts 15.22–31 Psalm 57.8–end John 15.12–17 *Lesser Festival eucharistic lectionary:* Isaiah 43.1–7 *or* Ecclesiasticus 2.10–17; Psalm 87; 2 Corinthians 4.5–12; John 12.20–26	Psalms **138**, 149 *or* **55** Numbers 14.1–25 Luke 6.1–11	Psalm **66** *or* **69** Deuteronomy 21.22—22.8 1 Peter 3.1–12
Saturday	**5 May**	*W*	Acts 16.1–10 Psalm 100 John 15.18–21	Psalms **146**, 150 *or* **76**, 79 Numbers 14.26–end Luke 6.12–26	Psalm **118** *or* 81, **84** Deuteronomy 24.5–end 1 Peter 3.13–end

Day	Date	Colour	Principal Service	3rd Service	2nd Service
Sunday	**6 May** **6th Sunday of Easter**	*W*	[Isaiah 55.1–11] Acts 10.44–end † Psalm 98 1 John 5.1–6 John 15.9–17 † *The reading from Acts must be used as either the first or second reading.*	Psalm 104.26–32 Ezekiel 47.1–12 John 21.1–19	Psalm 45 Song of Solomon 4.16—5.2; 8.6,7 Revelation 3.14–end *HC* Luke 22.24–30

Day	Date	Colour	Holy Communion	Morning Prayer	Evening Prayer
Monday	**7 May** Rogation Day	*W*	Acts 16.11–15 Psalm 149.1–5 John 15.26—16.4	Psalms **65**, 67 *or* **80**, 82 Numbers 16.1–35 Luke 6.27–38	Psalms **121**, 122, 123 *or* **85**, 86 Deuteronomy 26 1 Peter 4.1–11
Tuesday	**8 May** Julian of Norwich, spiritual writer, c.1417 (see p.84) Rogation Day	*W*	Acts 16.22–34 Psalm 138 John 16.5–11	Psalms 124, 125, **126**, 127 *or* 87, **89.1–18** Numbers 16.36–end Luke 6.39–end	Psalms **128**, 129, 130, 131 *or* **89.19–end** Deuteronomy 28.1–14 1 Peter 4.12–end
Wednesday	**9 May** Rogation Day	*W*	Acts 17.15, 22—18.1 Psalm 148.1–2, 11–end John 16.12–15	Psalms **132**, 133 *or* **119.105–128** Numbers 17.1–11 Luke 7.1–10	**1st EP of Ascension Day:** Psalms 15, 24 2 Samuel 23.1–5 Colossians 2.20—3.4

Day	Date	Colour	Principal Service	3rd Service	2nd Service
Thursday	**10 May** **Ascension Day**	*Gold or W*	Acts 1.1–11 † *or* Daniel 7.9–14 Psalm 47 *or* Psalm 93 Ephesians 1.15–end *or* Acts 1.1–11 † Luke 24.44–end † *The reading from Acts must be used as either the first or second reading.*	*MP* Psalms 110, 150 Isaiah 52.7–end Hebrews 7.[11–25] 26–end	*EP* Psalm 8 Song of the Three 29–37 *or* 2 Kings 2.1–15 Revelation 5 *HC* Matthew 28.16–end

The nine days after Ascension Day until the eve of Pentecost are observed as days of prayer and preparation for the celebration of the outpouring of the Holy Spirit.
*From 11–19 May, in preparation for the Day of Pentecost, an alternative sequence of daily readings for use at the one of the offices is marked with an asterisk *.*

Day	Date	Colour	Holy Communion	Morning Prayer	Evening Prayer
Friday	**11 May**	*W*	Acts 18.9–18 Psalm 47.1–6 John 16.20–23	Psalms 20, **81** *or* **88** (95) Numbers 20.1–13 Luke 7.11–17 **Exodus 35.30–36.1; Galatians 5.13–end*	Psalm **145**. *or* **102** Deuteronomy 29.2–15 1 John 1.1—2.6
Saturday	**12 May** *Gregory Dix, priest, monk, scholar, 1952*	*W*	Acts 18.22–end Psalm 47.1–2, 7–end John 16.23–28	Psalms 21, **47** *or* 96, **97**, 100 Numbers 21.4–9 Luke 7.18–35 **Numbers 11.16–17, 24–29; 1 Corinthians 2*	Psalms 84, **85** *or* **104** Deuteronomy 30 1 John 2.7–17

			Principal Service	3rd Service	2nd Service
Sunday	**13 May** **7th Sunday of Easter** *Sunday after Ascension Day*	*W*	[Ezekiel 36.24–28] Acts 1.15–17, 21–end † Psalm 1 1 John 5.9–13 John 17.6–19 † *The reading from Acts must be used as either the first or second reading.*	Psalm 76 Isaiah 14.3–15 Revelation 14.1–13	Psalm 147.1–12 Isaiah 61 Luke 4.14–21 *or:* 1st EP of Matthias the Apostle: Psalm 147 Isaiah 22.15–22 Philippians 3.13*b*—4.1
Monday	**14 May** Matthias the Apostle	*R*	Isaiah 22.15–end *or* Acts 1.15–end Psalm 15 Acts 1.15–end *or* 1 Corinthians 4.1–7 John 15.9–17	*MP* Psalms 16, 147.1–12 1 Samuel 2.27–35 Acts 2.37–end	*EP* Psalm 80 1 Samuel 16.1–13*a* Matthew 7.15–27
			Holy Communion	Morning Prayer	Evening Prayer
Tuesday	**15 May**	*W*	Acts 20.17–27 Psalm 68.9–10, 18–19 John 17.1–11	Psalms 98, **99**, 100 *or* **106*** (*or* 103) Numbers 22.36—23.12 Luke 8.1–15 **1 Samuel 10.1–10; 1 Corinthians 12.1–13*	Psalm **68** *or* **107*** Deuteronomy 31.14–29 1 John 3.1–10
Wednesday	**16 May** *Caroline Chisholm, social reformer, 1877*	*W*	Acts 20.28–end Psalm 68.27–28, 32–end John 17.11–19	Psalms 2, **29** *or* 110, **111**, 112 Numbers 23.13–end Luke 8.16–25 **1 Kings 19.1–18; Matthew 3.13–end*	Psalms 36, **46** *or* **119.129–152** Deuteronomy 31.30—32.14 1 John 3.11–end
Thursday	**17 May**	*W*	Acts 22.30; 23.6–11 Psalm 16.1, 5–end John 17.20–end	Psalms **24**, 72 *or* 113, **115** Numbers 24 Luke 8.26–39 **Ezekiel 11.14–20; Matthew 9.35—10.20*	Psalm **139** *or* 114, **116**, 117 Deuteronomy 32.15–47 1 John 4.1–6
Friday	**18 May**	*W*	Acts 25.13–21 Psalm 103.1–2, 11–12, 19–20 John 21.15–19	Psalms **28**, 30 *or* **139** Numbers 27.12–end Luke 8.40–end **Ezekiel 36.22–28; Matthew 12.22–32*	Psalm **147** *or* **130**, 131, 137 Deuteronomy 33 1 John 4.7–end
Saturday	**19 May** Dunstan, archbishop, monastic reformer, 988 (see p.83)	*W*	Acts 28.16–20, 30–end Psalm 11.4–end John 21.20–end	Psalms 42, **43** *or* 120, **121**, 122 Numbers 32.1–27 Luke 9.1–17 **Micah 3.1–8; Ephesians 6.10–20 (at MP only)*	**1st EP of Pentecost:** Psalm 48 Deuteronomy 16.9–15 John 7.37–39

Day	Date / Observance	Colour	Principal Service	3rd Service	2nd Service
Sunday	**20 May** **Pentecost** *Whit Sunday*	*R*	Acts 2.1–21 † *or* Ezekiel 37.1–14 Psalm 104.26–36, 37*b* [*or* 104.26–end] Romans 8.22–27 *or* Acts 2.1–21 † John 15.26–27; 16.4*b*–15 *† The reading from Acts must be used as either the first or second reading.*	*MP* Psalm 145 Isaiah 11.1–9 *or* Wisdom 7.15–23 [24–27] 1 Corinthians 12.4–13	*EP* Psalm 139.1–11 [13–18, 23–24] Ezekiel 36.22–28 Acts 2.22–38 *HC* John 20.19–23
			Holy Communion	**Morning Prayer**	**Evening Prayer**
Monday	**21 May** *Helena, protector of the Holy Places, 330* Ordinary Time resumes today DEL week 7	*G*	James 3.13–end Psalm 19.7–end Mark 9.14–29	Psalms 123, 124, 125, **126** Joshua 1 Luke 9.18–27	Psalms **127**, 128, 129 2 Chronicles 17.1–12 Romans 1.1–17
Tuesday	**22 May**	*G*	James 4.1–10 Psalm 55.7–9, 24 Mark 9.30–37	Psalms **132**, 133 Joshua 2 Luke 9.28–36	Psalms (134,) **135** 2 Chronicles 18.1–27 Romans 1.18–end
Wednesday	**23 May**	*G*	James 4.13–end Psalm 49.1–2, 5–10 Mark 9.38–40	Psalm **119.153–end** Joshua 3 Luke 9.37–50	Psalm **136** 2 Chronicles 18.28—end of 19 Romans 2.1–16
Thursday	**24 May** John and Charles Wesley, evangelists, hymn writers, 1791 and 1788 (see p.83)	*Gw*	James 5.1–6 Psalm 49.12–20 Mark 9.41–50	Psalms **143**, 146 Joshua 4.1—5.1 Luke 9.51–end	Psalms **138**, 140, 141 2 Chronicles 20.1–23 Romans 2.17–end
Friday	**25 May** The Venerable Bede, monk, scholar, historian, 735 (see p.84) *Aldhelm, bishop, 709*	*Gw*	James 5.9–12 Psalm 103.1–4, 8–13 Mark 10.1–12	Psalms 142, **144** Joshua 5.2–end Luke 10.1–16	Psalm 145 2 Chronicles 22.10—end of 23 Romans 3.1–20
Saturday	**26 May** Augustine, archbishop, 605 (see p.83) *John Calvin, reformer, 1564* *Philip Neri, founder of the Oratorians, spiritual guide, 1595*	*Gw*	James 5.13–end Psalm 141.1–4 Mark 10.13–16	Psalm **147** Joshua 6.1–20 Luke 10.17–24	**1st EP of Trinity Sunday:** Psalms 97, 98 Isaiah 40.12–end Mark 1.1–13

Day	Date	Colour	Principal Service	3rd Service	2nd Service
Sunday	**27 May** Trinity Sunday	*Gold or W*	Isaiah 6.1–8 Psalm 29 Romans 8.12–17 John 3.1–17	*MP* Psalm 33.1–12 Proverbs 8.1–4, 22–31 2 Corinthians 13.[5–10] 11–end	*EP* Psalm 104.1–10 Ezekiel 1.4–10, 22–28*a* Revelation 4 *HC* Mark 1.1–13
			Holy Communion	**Morning Prayer**	**Evening Prayer**
Monday	**28 May** *Lanfranc, monk, archbishop, scholar, 1089* DEL week 8	*G*	1 Peter 1.3–9 Psalm 111 Mark 10.17–27	Psalms **1**, 2, 3 Joshua 7.1–15 Luke 10.25–37	Psalms **4**, 7 2 Chronicles 26.1–21 Romans 4.1–12
Tuesday	**29 May**	*G*	1 Peter 1.10–16 Psalm 98.1–5 Mark 10.28–31	Psalms **5**, 6 (8) Joshua 7.16–end Luke 10.38–end	Psalms **9**, 10* 2 Chronicles 28 Romans 4.13–end
	If Corpus Christi is kept as a Festival:				
			Holy Communion	**Morning Prayer**	**Evening Prayer**
Wednesday	**30 May** Josephine Butler, social reformer, 1906 (see p.85) *Joan of Arc, visionary, 1431* *Apolo Kivebulaya, priest, evangelist, 1933*	*Gw*	1 Peter 1.18–end Psalm 147.13–end Mark 10.32–45	Psalm **119.1–32** Joshua 8.1–29 Luke 11.1–13	Psalms **11**, 12, 13 2 Chronicles 29.1–19 Romans 5.1–11 *or:* 1st EP of Corpus Christi: Psalms 110, 111 Exodus 16.2–15 John 6.22–35
			Principal Service	**3rd Service**	**2nd Service**
Thursday	**31 May** Day of Thanksgiving for the Institution of Holy Communion (Corpus Christi)	*W*	Genesis 14.18–20 Psalm 116.10–end 1 Corinthians 11.23–26 John 6.51–58	*MP* Psalm 147 Deuteronomy 8.2–16 1 Corinthians 10.1–17	*EP* Psalms 23, 42, 43 Proverbs 9.1–5 Luke 9.11–17
Friday	**1 June** Visit of the Blessed Virgin Mary to Elizabeth *(transferred from 31 May)*	*W*	Zephaniah 3.14–18 Psalm 113 Romans 12.9–16 Luke 1.39–49 [50–56]	*MP* Psalms 85, 150 1 Samuel 2.1–10 Mark 3.31–end	*EP* Psalms 122, 127, 128 Zechariah 2.10–end John 3.25–30
			Holy Communion	**Morning Prayer**	**Evening Prayer**
Saturday	**2 June**	*G*	Jude 17, 20–end Psalm 63.1–6 Mark 11.27–end	Psalms 20, 21, **23** Joshua 10.1–15 Luke 11.37–end	Psalms **24**, 25 2 Chronicles 32.1–22 Romans 6.15–end

If Corpus Christi is not kept as a Festival:

Day	Date		Holy Communion	Morning Prayer	Evening Prayer
Wednesday	**30 May** Josephine Butler, social reformer, 1906 (see p.85) *Joan of Arc, visionary, 1431* *Apolo Kivebulaya, priest, evangelist, 1933*	*Gw*	1 Peter 1.18–end Psalm 147.13–end Mark 10.32–45	Psalm **119.1–32** Joshua 8.1–29 Luke 11.1–13	Psalms **11**, 12, 13 2 Chronicles 29.1–19 Romans 5.1–11 *or:* 1st EP of the Visit of the BVM to Elizabeth: Psalm 45 Song of Solomon 2.8–14 Luke 1.26–38
			Principal Service	**3rd Service**	**2nd Service**
Thursday	**31 May** Visit of the Blessed Virgin Mary to Elizabeth	*W*	Zephaniah 3.14–18 Psalm 113 Romans 12.9–16 Luke 1.39–49 [50–56]	*MP* Psalms 85, 150 1 Samuel 2.1–10 Mark 3.31–end	*EP* Psalms 122, 127, 128 Zechariah 2.10–end John 3.25–30
			Holy Communion	**Morning Prayer**	**Evening Prayer**
Friday	**1 June** Justin, martyr, c.165 (see p.81)	*Gr*	1 Peter 4.7–13 Psalm 96.10–end Mark 11.11–26	Psalms 17, **19** Joshua 9.3–26 Luke 11.29–36	Psalm **22** 2 Chronicles 30 Romans 6.1–14
Saturday	**2 June**	*G*	Jude 17, 20–end Psalm 63.1–6 Mark 11.27–end	Psalms 20, 21, **23** Joshua 10.1–15 Luke 11.37–end	Psalms **24**, 25 2 Chronicles 32.1–22 Romans 6.15–end

		Principal Service	3rd Service	2nd Service
Sunday	**3 June** *G* **1st Sunday after Trinity** Proper 4	*Continuous:* 1 Samuel 3.1–10 [11–20] Psalm 139.1–5, 12–18 *Related:* Deuteronomy 5.12–15 Psalm 81.1–10 2 Corinthians 4.5–12 Mark 2.23—3.6	Psalms 28, 32 Deuteronomy 5.1–21 Acts 21.17–39*a*	Psalm 35 [*or* 35.1–10] Jeremiah 5.1–19 Romans 7.7–end *HC* Luke 7.1–10
		Holy Communion	**Morning Prayer**	**Evening Prayer**
Monday	**4 June** *G* *Petroc, abbot, 6th cent.* DEL week 9	2 Peter 1.2–7 Psalm 91.1–2, 14–end Mark 12.1–12	Psalms 27, **30** Joshua 14 Luke 12.1–12	Psalms 26, **28**, 29 2 Chronicles 33.1–13 Romans 7.1–6
Tuesday	**5 June** *Gr* Boniface (Wynfrith), bishop, martyr, 754 (see p.81)	2 Peter 3.11–15*a*, 17–end Psalm 90.1–4, 10, 14, 16 Mark 12.13–17	Psalms 32, **36** Joshua 21.43—22.8 Luke 12.13–21	Psalm **33** 2 Chronicles 34.1–18 Romans 7.7–end
Wednesday	**6 June** *G* *Ini Kopuria, founder of the Melanesian Brotherhood, 1945*	2 Timothy 1.1–3, 6–12 Psalm 123 Mark 12.18–27	Psalm **34** Joshua 22.9–end Luke 12.22–31	Psalm **119.33–56** 2 Chronicles 34.19–end Romans 8.1–11
Thursday	**7 June** *G*	2 Timothy 2.8–15 Psalm 25.4–12 Mark 12.28–34	Psalm **37*** Joshua 23 Luke 12.32–40	Psalms 39, **40** 2 Chronicles 35.1–19 Romans 8.12–17
Friday	**8 June** *Gw* Thomas Ken, bishop, nonjuror, hymn writer, 1711 (see p.83)	2 Timothy 3.10–end Psalm 119.161–168 Mark 12.35–37	Psalm **31** Joshua 24.1–28 Luke 12.41–48	Psalm **35** 2 Chronicles 35.20—36.10 Romans 8.18–30
Saturday	**9 June** *Gw* Columba, abbot, missionary, 597 (see p.84) *Ephrem, deacon, hymn writer, teacher of the faith, 373*	2 Timothy 4.1–8 Psalm 71.7–16 Mark 12.38–end	Psalms 41, **42**, 43 Joshua 24.29–end Luke 12.49–end	Psalms 45, **46** 2 Chronicles 36.11–end Romans 8.31–end

			Principal Service	3rd Service	2nd Service
Sunday	**10 June** **2nd Sunday after Trinity** Proper 5	*G*	*Continuous:* 1 Samuel 8.4–11 [12–15] 16–20; [11.14–end] Psalm 138 *Related:* Genesis 3.8–15 Psalm 130 2 Corinthians 4.13—5.1 Mark 3.20–end	Psalm 36 Deuteronomy 6.10–end Acts 22.22—23.11	Psalm 37.1–11[12–17] Jeremiah 6.16–21 Romans 9.1–13 *HC* Luke 7.11–17 *or:* 1st EP of Barnabas the Apostle: Psalms 1, 15 Isaiah 42.5–12 Acts 14.8–end
Monday	**11 June** Barnabas the Apostle	*R*	Job 29.11–16 *or* Acts 11.19–end Psalm 112 Acts 11.19–end *or* Galatians 2.1–10 John 15.12–17	*MP* Psalms 100, 101, 117 Jeremiah 9.23–24 Acts 4.32–end	*EP* Psalm 147 Ecclesiastes 12.9–end *or* Tobit 4.5–11 Acts 9.26–31
			Holy Communion	**Morning Prayer**	**Evening Prayer**
Tuesday	**12 June** DEL week 10	*G*	1 Kings 17.7–16 Psalm 4 Matthew 5.13–16	Psalms **48**, 52 Judges 4.1–23 Luke 13.10–21	Psalm **50** Ezra 3 Romans 9.19–end
Wednesday	**13 June**	*G*	1 Kings 18.20–39 Psalm 16.1, 6–end Matthew 5.17–19	Psalm **119.57–80** Judges 5 Luke 13.22–end	Psalms **59**, 60 (67) Ezra 4.1–5 Romans 10.1–10
Thursday	**14 June** *Richard Baxter, puritan divine, 1691*	*G*	1 Kings 18.41–end Psalm 65.8–end Matthew 5.20–26	Psalms 56, **57** (63*) Judges 6.1–24 Luke 14.1–11	Psalms 61, **62**, 64 Ezra 4.7–end Romans 10.11–end
Friday	**15 June** *Evelyn Underhill, spiritual writer, 1941*	*G*	1 Kings 19.9, 11–16 Psalm 27.8–16 Matthew 5.27–32	Psalms **51**, 54 Judges 6.25–end Luke 14.12–24	Psalm **38** Ezra 5 Romans 11.1–12
Saturday	**16 June** Richard, bishop, 1253 (see p.83) *Joseph Butler, bishop, philosopher, 1752*	*Gw*	1 Kings 19.19–end Psalm 16.1–7 Matthew 5.33–37	Psalm **68** Judges 7 Luke 14.25–end	Psalms 65, **66** Ezra 6 Romans 11.13–24

		Principal Service	3rd Service	2nd Service
Sunday	**17 June** *G* **3rd Sunday after Trinity** Proper 6	*Continuous:* 1 Samuel 15.34—16.13 Psalm 20 *Related:* Ezekiel 17.22–end Psalm 92.1–4,12–end [*or* 92.1–8] 2 Corinthians 5.6–10 [11–13] 14–17 Mark 4.26–34	Psalms 42, 43 Deuteronomy 10.12—11.1 Acts 23.12–35	Psalm 39 Jeremiah 7.1–16 Romans 9.14–26 *HC* Luke 7.36—8.3
		Holy Communion	**Morning Prayer**	**Evening Prayer**
Monday	**18 June** *G* *Bernard Mizeki, martyr, 1896* DEL week 11	1 Kings 21.1–16 Psalm 5.1–5 Matthew 5.38–42	Psalm **71** Judges 8.22–end Luke 15.1–10	Psalms **72**, 75 Ezra 7 Romans 11.25–end
Tuesday	**19 June** *G* *Sundar Singh, sadhu (holy man), evangelist, teacher of the faith, 1929*	1 Kings 21.17–end Psalm 51.1–9 Matthew 5.43–end	Psalm **73** Judges 9.1–21 Luke 15.11–end	Psalm **74** Ezra 8.15–end Romans 12.1–8
Wednesday	**20 June** *G*	2 Kings 2.1, 6–14 Psalm 31.21–end Matthew 6.1–6, 16–18	Psalm **77** Judges 9.22–end Luke 16.1–18	Psalm **119.81–104** Ezra 9 Romans 12.9–end
Thursday	**21 June** *G*	Ecclesiasticus 48.1–14 *or* Isaiah 63.7–9 Psalm 97.1–8 Matthew 6.7–15	Psalm **78.1–39*** Judges 11.1–11 Luke 16.19–end	Psalm **78.40–end*** Ezra 10.1–17 Romans 13.1–7
Friday	**22 June** *Gr* Alban, first martyr of Britain, c.250 (see p.81)	2 Kings 11.1–4, 9–18, 20 Psalm 132.1–5, 11–13 Matthew 6.19–23	Psalm **55** Judges 11.29–end Luke 17.1–10	Psalm **69** Nehemiah 1 Romans 13.8–end
Saturday	**23 June** *Gw* Etheldreda, abbess, c.678 (see p.84)	2 Chronicles 24.17–25 Psalm 89.25–33 Matthew 6.24–end	Psalms **76**, 79 Judges 12.1–7 Luke 17.11–19	Psalms 81, **84** Nehemiah 2 Romans 14.1–12 *or:* 1st EP of the Birth of John the Baptist: Psalm 71 Judges 13.2–7, 24–end Luke 1.5–25

Birth of John the Baptist / Trinity 4

If the Birth of John the Baptist *is celebrated on Sunday 24 June:*

			Principal Service	3rd Service	2nd Service
Sunday	**24 June** Birth of John the Baptist	*W*	Isaiah 40.1–11 Psalm 85.7–end Acts 13.14*b*–26 *or* Galatians 3.23–end Luke 1.57–66, 80	*MP* Psalms 50, 149 Ecclesiasticus 48.1–10 *or* Malachi 3.1–6 Luke 3.1–17	*EP* Psalms 80, 82 Malachi 4 Matthew 11.2–19
			Holy Communion	**Morning Prayer**	**Evening Prayer**
Monday	**25 June** DEL week 12	*G*	2 Kings 17.5–8, 13–15, 18 Psalm 60.1–5, 11–end Matthew 7.1–5	Psalms **80**, 82 Judges 13.1–24 Luke 17.20–end	Psalms **85**, 86 Nehemiah 4 Romans 14.13–end

If the Birth of John the Baptist *is transferred to Monday 25 June:*

			Principal Service		3rd Service	2nd Service
Sunday	**24 June** **4th Sunday after Trinity** Proper 7	*G*	*Continuous:* 1 Samuel 17. [1*a*,4–11, 19–23] 32–49 Psalm 9.9–end *or* 1 Samuel 17.57—18.5, 10–16 Psalm 133	*Related:* Job 38.1–11 Psalm 107.1–3, 23–32 [*or* 107.23–32]	Psalm 48 Deuteronomy 11.1–15 Acts 27.1–12	Psalm 49 Jeremiah 10.1–16 Romans 11.25–end *HC* Luke 8.26–39 *or:* 1st EP of the Birth of John the Baptist: Psalm 71 Judges 13.2–7, 24–end Luke 1.5–25
			2 Corinthians 6.1–13 Mark 4.35–end			
Monday	**25 June** Birth of John the Baptist *(transferred from 24 June)*	*W*	Isaiah 40.1–11 Psalm 85.7–end Acts 13.14*b*–26 *or* Galatians 3.23–end Luke 1.57–66, 80		*MP* Psalms 50, 149 Ecclesiasticus 48.1–10 *or* Malachi 3.1–6 Luke 3.1–17	*EP* Psalms 80, 82 Malachi 4 Matthew 11.2–19

			Holy Communion		Morning Prayer	Evening Prayer
Tuesday	**26 June** DEL week 12	*G*	2 Kings 19.9*b*–11, 14–21, 31–36 Psalm 48.1–2, 8–end Matthew 7.6, 12–14		Psalms 87, **89.1–18** Judges 14 Luke 18.1–14	Psalm **89.19–end** Nehemiah 5 Romans 15.1–13
Wednesday	**27 June** *Cyril, bishop, teacher of the faith, 444* Ember Day	*G*	2 Kings 22.8–13; 23.1–3 Psalm 119.33–40 Matthew 7.15–20		Psalm **119.105–128** Judges 15.1—16.3 Luke 18.15–30	Psalms **91**, 93 Nehemiah 6.1—7.4 Romans 15.14–21
Thursday	**28 June** Irenaeus, bishop, teacher of the faith, 200 (see p.82)	*Gw*	2 Kings 24.8–17 Psalm 79.1–9, 12 Matthew 7.21–end		Psalms 90, **92** Judges 16.4–end Luke 18.31–end	Psalm **94** Nehemiah 7.73*b*—end of 8 Romans 15.22–end
					or: 1st EP of Peter and Paul, Apostles [*or* †Peter the Apostle alone]:	Psalms 66, 67 Ezekiel 3.4–11 Galatians 1.13—2.8 [†Acts 9.32–end]
			Principal Service		**3rd Service**	**2nd Service**
Friday	**29 June** Peter and Paul, Apostles *or* Peter the Apostle Ember Day	*R* *R*	*Peter and Paul:* Zechariah 4.1–6*a*, 10*b*–end *or* Acts 12.1–11 Psalm 125 Acts 12.1–11 *or* 2 Timothy 4.6–8, 17–18 Matthew 16.13–19	*Peter alone:* Ezekiel 3.22–end *or* Acts 12.1–11 Psalm 125 Acts 12.1–11 *or* 1 Peter 2.19–end Matthew 16.13–19	*MP* Psalms 71, 113 Isaiah 49.1–6 Acts 11.1–18	*EP* Psalms 124, 138 Ezekiel 34.11–16 John 21.15–22
			Holy Communion		**Morning Prayer**	**Evening Prayer**
Saturday	**30 June** Ember Day	*G*	Lamentations 2.2, 10–14, 18–19 Psalm 74.1–3, 21–end Matthew 8.5–17		Psalms 96, **97**, 100 Judges 18.1–20, 27–end Luke 19.11–27	Psalm **104** Nehemiah 9.24–end Romans 16.17–end

Day	Date		Principal Service		3rd Service	2nd Service
Sunday	**1 July** **5th Sunday after Trinity** Proper 8	*G*	*Continuous* 2 Samuel 1.1, 17–end Psalm 130	*Related:* Wisdom 1.13–15; 2.23–24 *Canticle*: Lamentations 3.23–33 *or* Psalm 30 *† Lamentations 3.23–33 may be read as the first reading in place of Wisdom 1.13–15; 2.23–24*	Psalm 56 Deuteronomy 15.1–11 Acts 27.[13–32] 33–end	Psalms [52] 53 Jeremiah 11.1–14 Romans 13.1–10
			2 Corinthians 8.7–end Mark 5.21–end			
			Holy Communion		**Morning Prayer**	**Evening Prayer**
Monday	**2 July** DEL week 13	*G*	Amos 2.6–10, 13–end Psalm 50.16–23 Matthew 8.18–22		Psalms **98**, 99, 101 1 Samuel 1.1–20 Luke 19.28–40	Psalm **105*** (*or* 103) Nehemiah 12.27–47 2 Corinthians 1.1–14 *or:* 1st EP of Thomas the Apostle: Psalm 27 Isaiah 35 Hebrews 10.35—11.1
			Principal Service		**3rd Service**	**2nd Service**
Tuesday	**3 July** Thomas the Apostle	*R*	Habakkuk 2.1–4 Psalm 31.1–6 Ephesians 2.19–end John 20.24–29		*MP* Psalms 92, 146 2 Samuel 15.17–21 *or* Ecclesiasticus 2 John 11.1–16	*EP* Psalm 139 Job 42.1–6 1 Peter 1.3–12
			Holy Communion		**Morning Prayer**	**Evening Prayer**
Wednesday	**4 July**	*G*	Amos 5.14–15, 21–24 Psalm 50.7–14 Matthew 8.28–end		Psalms 110, **111**, 112 1 Samuel 2.12–26 Luke 20.1–8	Psalm **119.129–152** Nehemiah 13.15–end 2 Corinthians 2.5–end
Thursday	**5 July**	*G*	Amos 7.10–end Psalm 19.7–10 Matthew 9.1–8		Psalms 113, **115** 1 Samuel 2.27–end Luke 20.9–19	Psalms 114, **116**, 117 Esther 1 2 Corinthians 3
Friday	**6 July** *Thomas More, scholar, and John Fisher, bishop, martyrs, 1535*	*G*	Amos 8.4–6, 9–12 Psalm 119.1–8 Matthew 9.9–13		Psalm **139** 1 Samuel 3.1—4.1*a* Luke 20.20–26	Psalms **130**, 131, 137 Esther 2 2 Corinthians 4
Saturday	**7 July**	*G*	Amos 9.11–end Psalm 85.8–end Matthew 9.14–17		Psalms 120, **121**, 122 1 Samuel 4.1*b*–end Luke 20.27–40	Psalm **118** Esther 3 2 Corinthians 5

			Principal Service		3rd Service	2nd Service
Sunday	**8 July** **6th Sunday after Trinity** Proper 9	*G*	*Continuous:* 2 Samuel 5.1–5, 9–10 Psalm 48 2 Corinthians 12.2–10 Mark 6.1–13	*Related:* Ezekiel 2.1–5 Psalm 123	Psalm 57 Deuteronomy 24.10–end Acts 28.1–16	Psalms [63] 64 Jeremiah 20.1–11*a* Romans 14.1–17 *HC* Luke 10.1–11, 16–20
			Holy Communion		Morning Prayer	Evening Prayer
Monday	**9 July** DEL week 14	*G*	Hosea 2.14–16, 19–20 Psalm 145.2–9 Matthew 9.18–26		Psalms 123, 124, 125, **126** 1 Samuel 5 Luke 20.41—21.4	Psalms **127**, 128, 129 Esther 4 2 Corinthians 6.1—7.1
Tuesday	**10 July**	*G*	Hosea 8.4–7, 11–13 Psalm 103.8–12 Matthew 9.32–end		Psalms **132**, 133 1 Samuel 6.1–16 Luke 21.5–19	Psalms (134,) **135** Esther 5 2 Corinthians 7.2–end
Wednesday	**11 July** Benedict, abbot, c.550 (see p.84)	*Gw*	Hosea 10.1–3, 7–8, 12 Psalm 115.3–10 Matthew 10.1–7		Psalm **119.153–end** 1 Samuel 7 Luke 21.20–28	Psalm **136** Esther 6.1–13 2 Corinthians 8.1–15
Thursday	**12 July**	*G*	Hosea 11.1, 3–4, 8–9 Psalm 105.1–7 Matthew 10.7–15		Psalms **143**, 146 1 Samuel 8 Luke 21.29–end	Psalms **138**, 140, 141 Esther 6.14—end of 7 2 Corinthians 8.16—9.5
Friday	**13 July**	*G*	Hosea 14.2–end Psalm 80.1–7 Matthew 10.16–23		Psalms 142, **144** 1 Samuel 9.1–14 Luke 22.1–13	Psalm **145** Esther 8 2 Corinthians 9.6–end
Saturday	**14 July** John Keble, priest, poet, 1866 (see p.83)	*Gw*	Isaiah 6.1–8 Psalm 51.1–7 Matthew 10.24–33		Psalm **147** 1 Samuel 9.15—10.1 Luke 22.14–23	Psalms **148**, 149, 150 Esther 9.20–28 2 Corinthians 10

			Principal Service	3rd Service	2nd Service
Sunday	**15 July** **7th Sunday after Trinity** Proper 10	*G*	*Continuous:* 2 Samuel 6.1–5, 12*b*–19 Psalm 24 *Related:* Amos 7.7–15 Psalm 85.8–end Ephesians 1.3–14 Mark 6.14–29	Psalm 65 Deuteronomy 28.1–14 Acts 28.17–end	Psalm 66 [*or* 66.1–8] Job 4.1; 5.6–end *or* Ecclesiasticus 4.11–end Romans 15.14–29 *HC* Luke 10.25–37
			Holy Communion	**Morning Prayer**	**Evening Prayer**
Monday	**16 July** *Osmund, bishop, 1099* DEL week 15	*G*	Isaiah 1.11–17 Psalm 50.7–15 Matthew 10.34—11.1	Psalms **1**, 2, 3 1 Samuel 10.1–16 Luke 22.24–30	Psalms **4**, 7 Jeremiah 26 2 Corinthians 11.1–15
Tuesday	**17 July**	*G*	Isaiah 7.1–9 Psalm 48.1–7 Matthew 11.20–24	Psalms **5**, 6 (8) 1 Samuel 10.17–end Luke 22.31–38	Psalms **9**, 10* Jeremiah 28 2 Corinthians 11.16–end
Wednesday	**18 July** *Elizabeth Ferard, deaconess, founder of the Community of St Andrew, 1883*	*G*	Isaiah 10.5–7, 13–16 Psalm 94.5–11 Matthew 11.25–27	Psalm **119.1–32** 1 Samuel 11 Luke 22.39–46	Psalms **11**, 12, 13 Jeremiah 29.1–14 2 Corinthians 12
Thursday	**19 July** Gregory, bishop, and his sister Macrina, deaconess, teachers of the faith, c.394 and c.379 (see p.82)	*Gw*	Isaiah 26.7–9, 16–19 Psalm 102.14–21 Matthew 11.28–end	Psalms 14, **15**, 16 1 Samuel 12 Luke 22.47–62	Psalm **18*** Jeremiah 30.1–11 2 Corinthians 13
Friday	**20 July** *Margaret of Antioch, martyr, 4th cent.* *Bartolomé de las Casas, Apostle to the Indies, 1566*	*G*	Isaiah 38.1–6, 21–22, 7–8 [*sic*] *Canticle:* Isaiah 38.10–16 *or* Psalm 32.1–8 Matthew 12.1–8	Psalms 17, **19** 1 Samuel 13.5–18 Luke 22.63–end	Psalm **22** Jeremiah 30.12–22 James 1.1–11
Saturday	**21 July**	*G*	Micah 2.1–5 Psalm 10.1–5*a*, 12 Matthew 12.14–21	Psalms 20, 21, **23** 1 Samuel 13.19—14.15 Luke 23.1–12	Psalms **24**, 25 Jeremiah 31.1–22 James 1.12–end *or:* 1st EP of Mary Magdalene: Psalm 139 Isaiah 25.1–9 2 Corinthians 1.3–7

If Mary Magdalene *is celebrated on Sunday 22 July:*

Day	Date	Colour	Principal Service	3rd Service	2nd Service
Sunday	**22 July** Mary Magdalene	*W*	Song of Solomon 3.1–4 Psalm 42.1–10 2 Corinthians 5.14–17 John 20.1–2, 11–18	*MP* Psalms 30, 32, 150 1 Samuel 16.14–end Luke 8.1–3	*EP* Psalm 63 Zephaniah 3.14–end Mark 15.40—16.7
			Holy Communion	**Morning Prayer**	**Evening Prayer**
Monday	**23 July** *Bridget, abbess, 1373* DEL week 16	*G*	Micah 6.1–4, 6–8 Psalm 50.3–7, 14 Matthew 12.38–42	Psalms 27, **30** 1 Samuel 14.24–46 Luke 23.13–25	Psalms 26, **28**, 29 Jeremiah 31.23–25, 27–37 James 2.1–13

If Mary Magdalene *is transferred to Monday 23 July:*

Day	Date	Colour	Principal Service	3rd Service	2nd Service
Sunday	**22 July** **8th Sunday after Trinity** Proper 11	*G*	*Continuous:* 2 Samuel 7.1–14*a*; Psalm 89.20–37 *Related:* Jeremiah 23.1–6; Psalm 23 Ephesians 2.11–end Mark 6.30–34, 53–end	Psalms 67, 70 Deuteronomy 30.1–10 1 Peter 3.8–18	Psalm 73 [*or* 73.21–end] Job 13.13—14.6 *or* Ecclesiasticus 18.1–14 Hebrews 2.5–end *HC* Luke 10.38–end *or:* 1st EP of Mary Magdalene: Psalm 139 Isaiah 25.1–9 2 Corinthians 1.3–7
Monday	**23 July** Mary Magdalene *(transferred from 22 July)*	*W*	Song of Solomon 3.1–4 Psalm 42.1–10 2 Corinthians 5.14–17 John 20.1–2, 11–18	*MP* Psalms 30, 32, 150 1 Samuel 16.14–end Luke 8.1–3	*EP* Psalm 63 Zephaniah 3.14–end Mark 15.40—16.7

			Holy Communion	Morning Prayer	Evening Prayer
Tuesday	**24 July** DEL week 16	*G*	Micah 7.14–15, 18–20 Psalm 85.1–7 Matthew 12.46–end	Psalms 32, **36** 1 Samuel 15.1–23 Luke 23.26–43	Psalm **33** Jeremiah 32.1–15 James 2.14–end *or:* 1st EP of James the Apostle: Psalm 144 Deuteronomy 30.11–end Mark 5.21–end
			Principal Service	**3rd Service**	**2nd Service**
Wednesday	**25 July** James the Apostle	*R*	Jeremiah 45.1–5 *or* Acts 11.27—12.2 Psalm 126 Acts 11.27—12.2 *or* 2 Corinthians 4.7–15 Matthew 20.20–28	*MP* Psalms 7, 29, 117 2 Kings 1.9–15 Luke 9.46–56	*EP* Psalm 94 Jeremiah 26.1–15 Mark 1.14–20
			Holy Communion	**Morning Prayer**	**Evening Prayer**
Thursday	**26 July** Anne and Joachim, parents of the Blessed Virgin Mary	*Gw*	Jeremiah 2.1–3, 7–8, 12–13 Psalm 36.5–10 Matthew 13.10–17 *Lesser Festival eucharistic lectionary:* Zephaniah 3.14–18*a* Psalm 127 Romans 8.28–30 Matthew 13.16–17	Psalm **37*** 1 Samuel 17.1–30 Luke 23.56*b*—24.12	Psalms 39, **40** Jeremiah 33.14–end James 4.1–12
Friday	**27 July** *Brooke Foss Westcott, bishop, teacher of the faith, 1901*	*G*	Jeremiah 3.14–17 Psalm 23 *or Canticle:* Jeremiah 31.10–13 Matthew 13.18–23	Psalm **31** 1 Samuel 17.31–54 Luke 24.13–35	Psalm **35** Jeremiah 35 James 4.13—5.6
Saturday	**28 July**	*G*	Jeremiah 7.1–11 Psalm 84.1–6 Matthew 13.24–30	Psalms 41, **42**, 43 1 Samuel 17.55—18.16 Luke 24.36–end	Psalms 45, **46** Jeremiah 36.1–18 James 5.7–end

		Principal Service	3rd Service	2nd Service
Sunday	**29 July** *G* **9th Sunday after Trinity** Proper 12	*Continuous:* 2 Samuel 11.1–15; Psalm 14 *Related:* 2 Kings 4.42–end; Psalm 145.10–19 Ephesians 3.14–end John 6.1–21	Psalm 75 Song of Solomon 2 *or* 1 Maccabees 2.[1–14] 15–22 1 Peter 4.7–14	Psalm 74 [*or* 74.11–16] Job 19.1–27*a* *or* Ecclesiasticus 38.24–end Hebrews 8 *HC* Luke 11.1–13
		Holy Communion	Morning Prayer	Evening Prayer
Monday	**30 July** *Gw* William Wilberforce, social reformer, Olaudah Equiano and Thomas Clarkson, anti-slavery campaigners, 1833, 1797 and 1846 (see p.85) DEL week 17	Jeremiah 13.1–11 Psalm 82 *or* Deuteronomy 32.18–21 Matthew 13.31–35	Psalm **44** 1 Samuel 19.1–18 Acts 1.1–14	Psalms **47**, 49 Jeremiah 36.19–end Mark 1.1–13
Tuesday	**31 July** *G* *Ignatius of Loyola, founder of the Society of Jesus, 1556*	Jeremiah 14.17–end Psalm 79.8–end Matthew 13.36–43	Psalms **48**, 52 1 Samuel 20.1–17 Acts 1.15–end	Psalm **50** Jeremiah 37 Mark 1.14–20
Wednesday	**1 August** *G*	Jeremiah 15.10, 16–end Psalm 59.1–4, 18–end Matthew 13.44–46	Psalm **119.57–80** 1 Samuel 20.18–end Acts 2.1–21	Psalms **59**, 60 (67) Jeremiah 38.1–13 Mark 1.21–28
Thursday	**2 August** *G*	Jeremiah 18.1–6 Psalm 146.1–5 Matthew 13.47–53	Psalms 56, **57** (63*) 1 Samuel 21.1—22.5 Acts 2.22–36	Psalms 61, **62**, 64 Jeremiah 38.14–end Mark 1.29–end
Friday	**3 August** *G*	Jeremiah 26.1–9 Psalm 69.4–10 Matthew 13.54–end	Psalms **51**, 54 1 Samuel 22.6–end Acts 2.37–end	Psalm **38** Jeremiah 39 Mark 2.1–12
Saturday	**4 August** *G* *Jean-Baptiste Vianney, curé d'Ars, spiritual guide, 1859*	Jeremiah 26.11–16` Psalm 69.14–20 Matthew 14.1–12	Psalm **68** 1 Samuel 23 Acts 3.1–10	Psalms 65, **66** Jeremiah 40 Mark 2.13–22

		Principal Service	3rd Service	2nd Service
Sunday	**5 August** *G* **10th Sunday after Trinity** Proper 13	*Continuous:* 2 Samuel 11.26—12.13*a*; Psalm 51.1–13 *Related:* Exodus 16.2–4, 9–15; Psalm 78.23–29 Ephesians 4.1–16 John 6.24–35	Psalm 86 Song of Solomon 5.2–end *or* 1 Maccabees 3.1–12 2 Peter 1.1–15	Psalm 88 [*or* 88.1–10] Job 28 *or* Ecclesiasticus 42.15–end Hebrews 11.17–31 *HC* Luke 12.13–21 *or:* 1st EP of the Transfiguration of Our Lord: Psalms 99, 110 Exodus 24.12–end John 12.27–36*a*
Monday	**6 August** *Gold or W* Transfiguration of Our Lord	Daniel 7.9–10, 13–14 Psalm 97 2 Peter 1.16–19 Luke 9.28–36	*MP* Psalms 27, 150 Ecclesiasticus 48.1–10 *or* 1 Kings 19.1–16 1 John 3.1–3	*EP* Psalm 72 Exodus 34.29–end 2 Corinthians 3
		Holy Communion	**Morning Prayer**	**Evening Prayer**
Tuesday	**7 August** *G* *John Mason Neale, priest, hymn writer, 1866* DEL week 18	Jeremiah 30.1–2, 12–15, 18–22 Psalm 102.16–21 Matthew 14.22–end *or* 15.1–2, 10–14	Psalm **73** 1 Samuel 26 Acts 4.1–12	Psalm **74** Jeremiah 42 Mark 3.7–19*a*
Wednesday	**8 August** *Gw* Dominic, priest, founder of the Order of Preachers, 1221 (see p.84)	Jeremiah 31.1–7 Psalm 121 Matthew 15.21–28	Psalm **77** 1 Samuel 28.3–end Acts 4.13–31	Psalm **119.81–104** Jeremiah 43 Mark 3.19*b*–end
Thursday	**9 August** *Gw* Mary Sumner, founder of the Mothers' Union, 1921 (see p.85)	Jeremiah 31.31–34 Psalm 51.11–18 Matthew 16.13–23	Psalm **78.1–39*** 1 Samuel 31 Acts 4.32—5.11	Psalm **78.40–end*** Jeremiah 44.1–14 Mark 4.1–20
Friday	**10 August** *Gr* Laurence, deacon, martyr, 258 (see p.81)	Nahum 2.1, 3; 3.1–3, 6–7 Psalm 137.1–6 *or* Deuteronomy 32.35–36, 39, 41 Matthew 16.24–28	Psalm **55** 2 Samuel 1 Acts 5.12–26	Psalm **69** Jeremiah 44.15–end Mark 4.21–34
Saturday	**11 August** *Gw* Clare of Assisi, founder of the Poor Clares, 1253 (see p.84) *John Henry Newman, priest, 1890*	Habakkuk 1.12—2.4 Psalm 9.7–11 Matthew 17.14–20	Psalms **76**, 79 2 Samuel 2.1–11 Acts 5.27–end	Psalms 81, **84** Jeremiah 45 Mark 4.35–end

Day	Date	Principal Service	3rd Service	2nd Service
Sunday	**12 August** *G* **11th Sunday after Trinity** Proper 14	*Continuous:* 2 Samuel 18.5–9, 15, 31–33 Psalm 130 *Related:* 1 Kings 19.4–8 Psalm 34.1–8 Ephesians 4.25—5.2 John 6.35, 41–51	Psalm 90 Song of Solomon 8.5–7 *or* 1 Maccabees 14.4–15 2 Peter 3.8–13	Psalm 91 [*or* 91.1–12] Job 39.1—40.4 *or* Ecclesiasticus 43.13–end Hebrews 12.1–17 *HC* Luke 12.32–40
		Holy Communion	**Morning Prayer**	**Evening Prayer**
Monday	**13 August** *Gw* Jeremy Taylor, bishop, teacher of the faith, 1667 (see p.82) *Florence Nightingale, nurse, social reformer, 1910* *Octavia Hill, social reformer, 1912* DEL week 19	Ezekiel 1.2–5, 24–end Psalm 148.1–4, 12–13 Matthew 17.22–end	Psalms **80**, 82 2 Samuel 3.12–end Acts 6	Psalms **85**, 86 Micah 1.1–9 Mark 5.1–20
Tuesday	**14 August** *G* *Maximilian Kolbe, friar, martyr, 1941*	Ezekiel 2.8—3.4 Psalm 119.65–72 Matthew 18.1–5, 10, 12–14	Psalms 87, **89.1–18** 2 Samuel 5.1–12 Acts 7.1–16	Psalm **89.19–end** Micah 2 Mark 5.21–34 *or:* 1st EP of the Blessed Virgin Mary: Psalm 72 Proverbs 8.22–31 John 19.23–27
		Principal Service	**3rd Service**	**2nd Service**
Wednesday	**15 August** *W* The Blessed Virgin Mary	Isaiah 61.10–end *or* Revelation 11.19—12.6, 10 Psalm 45.10–end Galatians 4.4–7 Luke 1.46–55	*MP* Psalms 98, 138, 147.1–12 Isaiah 7.10–15 Luke 11.27–28	*EP* Psalm 132 Song of Solomon 2.1–7 Acts 1.6–14
		Holy Communion	**Morning Prayer**	**Evening Prayer**
Thursday	**16 August** *G*	Ezekiel 12.1–12 Psalm 78.58–64 Matthew 18.21—19.1	Psalms 90, **92** 2 Samuel 7.1–17 Acts 7.44–53	Psalm **94** Micah 4.1—5.1 Mark 6.1–13
Friday	**17 August** *G*	Ezekiel 16.1–15, 60–end Psalm 118.14–18 *or Canticle:* Song of Deliverance Matthew 19.3–12	Psalms **88** (95) 2 Samuel 7.18–end Acts 7.54—8.3	Psalm **102** Micah 5.2–end Mark 6.14–29
Saturday	**18 August** *G*	Ezekiel 18.1–11*a*, 13*b*, 30, 32 Psalm 51.1–3, 15–17 Matthew 19.13–15	Psalms 96, **97**, 100 2 Samuel 9 Acts 8.4–25	Psalm **104** Micah 6 Mark 6.30–44

			Principal Service	3rd Service	2nd Service
Sunday	**19 August** **12th Sunday after Trinity** Proper 15	*G*	*Continuous:* 1 Kings 2.10–12; 3.3–14 Psalm 111 *Related:* Proverbs 9.1–6 Psalm 34.9–14 Ephesians 5.15–20 John 6.51–58	Psalm 106.1–10 Jonah 1 *or* Ecclesiasticus 3.1–15 2 Peter 3.14–end	Psalms [92] 100 Exodus 2.23—3.10 Hebrews 13.1–15 *HC* Luke 12.49–56
			Holy Communion	**Morning Prayer**	**Evening Prayer**
Monday	**20 August** Bernard, abbot, teacher of the faith, 1153 (see p.82) *William and Catherine Booth, founders of the Salvation Army, 1912, 1890* DEL week 20	*Gw*	Ezekiel 24.15–24 Psalm 78.1–8 Matthew 19.16–22	Psalms **98**, 99, 101 2 Samuel 11 Acts 8.26–end	Psalm **105*** (*or* 103) Micah 7.1–7 Mark 6.45–end
Tuesday	**21 August**	*G*	Ezekiel 28.1–10 Psalm 107.1–3, 40, 43 Matthew 19.23–end	Psalm **106*** (*or* 103) 2 Samuel 12.1–25 Acts 9.1–19*a*	Psalm **107*** Micah 7.8–end Mark 7.1–13
Wednesday	**22 August**	*G*	Ezekiel 34.1–11 Psalm 23 Matthew 20.1–16	Psalms 110, **111**, 112 2 Samuel 15.1–12 Acts 9.19*b*–31	Psalm **119.129–152** Habakkuk 1.1–11 Mark 7.14–23
Thursday	**23 August**	*G*	Ezekiel 36.23–28 Psalm 51.7–12 Matthew 22.1–14	Psalms 113, **115** 2 Samuel 15.13–end Acts 9.32–end	Psalms 114, **116**, 117 Habakkuk 1.12—2.5 Mark 7.24–30 *or:* 1st EP of Bartholomew the Apostle: Psalm 97; Isaiah 61.1–9; 2 Corinthians 6.1–10
			Principal Service	**3rd Service**	**2nd Service**
Friday	**24 August** Bartholomew the Apostle	*R*	Isaiah 43.8–13 *or* Acts 5.12–16 Psalm 145.1–7 Acts 5.12–16 *or* 1 Corinthians 4.9–15 Luke 22.24–30	*MP* Psalms 86, 117 Genesis 28.10–17 John 1.43–end	*EP* Psalms 91, 116 Ecclesiasticus 39.1–10 *or* Deuteronomy 18.15–19 Matthew 10.1–22
			Holy Communion	**Morning Prayer**	**Evening Prayer**
Saturday	**25 August**	*G*	Ezekiel 43.1–7 Psalm 85.7–end Matthew 23.1–12	Psalms 120, **121**, 122 2 Samuel 17.1–23 Acts 10.17–33	Psalm **118** Habakkuk 3.2–19*a* Mark 8.1–10

		Principal Service	3rd Service	2nd Service
Sunday	**26 August** *G* **13th Sunday after Trinity** Proper 16	*Continuous:* 1 Kings 8.[1, 6, 10–11] 22–30, 41–43 Psalm 84 *Related:* Joshua 24.1–2*a*, 14–18 Psalm 34.15–end Ephesians 6.10–20 John 6.56–69	Psalm 115 Jonah 2 *or* Ecclesiasticus 3.17–29 Revelation 1	Psalm 116 [*or* 116.10–end] Exodus 4.27—5.1 Hebrews 13.16–21 *HC* Luke 13.10–17
		Holy Communion	**Morning Prayer**	**Evening Prayer**
Monday	**27 August** *Gw* Monica, mother of Augustine of Hippo, 387 (see p.85) DEL week 21	2 Thessalonians 1.1–5, 11–end Psalm 39.1–9 Matthew 23.13–22	Psalms 123, 124, 125, **126** 2 Samuel 18.1–18 Acts 10.34–end	Psalms **127**, 128, 129 Haggai 1.1–11 Mark 8.11–21
Tuesday	**28 August** *Gw* Augustine, bishop, teacher of the faith, 430 (see p.82)	2 Thessalonians 2.1–3*a*, 14–end Psalm 98 Matthew 23.23–26	Psalms **132**, 133 2 Samuel 18.19–19.8*a* Acts 11.1–18	Psalms (134,) **135** Haggai 1.12—2.9 Mark 8.22–26
Wednesday	**29 August** *Gr* Beheading of John the Baptist	2 Thessalonians 3.6–10, 16–end Psalm 128 Matthew 23.27–32 *Lesser Festival eucharistic lectionary:* Jeremiah 1.4–10 Psalm 11 Hebrews 11.32—12.2 Matthew 14.1–12	Psalm **119.153–end** 2 Samuel 19.8*b*–23 Acts 11.19–end	Psalm **136** Haggai 2.10–end Mark 8.27—9.1
Thursday	**30 August** *Gw* John Bunyan, spiritual writer, 1688 (see p.82)	1 Corinthians 1.1–9 Psalm 145.1–7 Matthew 24.42–end	Psalms **143**, 146 2 Samuel 19.24–end Acts 12.1–17	Psalms **138**, 140, 141 Zechariah 1.1–17 Mark 9.2–13
Friday	**31 August** *Gw* Aidan, bishop, missionary, 651 (see p.84)	1 Corinthians 1.17–25 Psalm 33.6–12 Matthew 25.1–13	Psalms 142, **144** 2 Samuel 23.1–7 Acts 12.18–end	Psalm **145** Zechariah 1.18—end of 2 Mark 9.14–29
Saturday	**1 September** *G* *Giles, hermit, c.710*	1 Corinthians 1.26–end Psalm 33.12–15, 20–end Matthew 25.14–30	Psalm **147** 2 Samuel 24 Acts 13.1–12	Psalms **148**, 149, 150 Zechariah 3 Mark 9.30–37

		Principal Service	3rd Service	2nd Service
Sunday	**2 September** *G* **14th Sunday after Trinity** Proper 17	*Continuous:* Song of Solomon 2.8–13 Psalm 45.1–2, 6–9 [*or* 45.1–7] *Related:* Deuteronomy 4.1–2, 6–9 Psalm 15 James 1.17–end Mark 7.1–8, 14, 15, 21–23	Psalm 119.17–40 Jonah 3.1–9 *or* Ecclesiasticus 11.7–28 (*or* 19–28) Revelation 3.14–end	Psalm 119.1–16 [*or* 119.9–16] Exodus 12.21–27 Matthew 4.23—5.20
		Holy Communion	**Morning Prayer**	**Evening Prayer**
Monday	**3 September** *Gw* Gregory the Great, bishop, teacher of the faith, 604 (see p.82) DEL week 22	1 Corinthians 2.1–5 Psalm 33.12–21 Luke 4.16–30	Psalms **1**, 2, 3 1 Kings 1.5–31 Acts 13.13–43	Psalms **4**, 7 Zechariah 4 Mark 9.38–end
Tuesday	**4 September** *G* *Birinus, bishop, 650*	1 Corinthians 2.10*b*–end Psalm 145.10–17 Luke 4.31–37	Psalms **5**, 6 (8) 1 Kings 1.32—2.4, 2.10–12 Acts 13.44—14.7	Psalms **9**, 10* Zechariah 6.9–end Mark 10.1–16
Wednesday	**5 September** *G*	1 Corinthians 3.1–9 Psalm 62 Luke 4.38–end	Psalm **119.1–32** 1 Kings 3 Acts 14.8–end	Psalms **11**, 12, 13 Zechariah 7 Mark 10.17–31
Thursday	**6 September** *G* *Allen Gardiner, missionary, founder of the South American Mission Society, 1851*	1 Corinthians 3.18–end Psalm 24.1–6 Luke 5.1–11	Psalms 14, **15**, 16 1 Kings 4.29—5.12 Acts 15.1–21	Psalm **18*** Zechariah 8.1–8 Mark 10.32–34
Friday	**7 September** *G*	1 Corinthians 4.1–5 Psalm 37.3–8 Luke 5.33–end	Psalms 17, **19** 1 Kings 6.1, 11–28 Acts 15.22–35	Psalm **22** Zechariah 8.9–end Mark 10.35–45
Saturday	**8 September** *Gw* Birth of the Blessed Virgin Mary (see p.81)	1 Corinthians 4.6–15 Psalm 145.18–end Luke 6.1–5	Psalms 20, 21, **23** 1 Kings 8.1–30 Acts 15.36—16.5	Psalms **24**, 25 Zechariah 9.1–12 Mark 10.46–end

If the Festival of the Blessed Virgin Mary *is transferred to 8 September, the provision (including 1st EP) for 15 August is used.*

			Principal Service	3rd Service	2nd Service
Sunday	**9 September** **15th Sunday after Trinity** Proper 18	*G*	*Continuous:* Proverbs 22.1–2, 8, 9, 22, 23 Psalm 125 *Related:* Isaiah 35.4–7*a* Psalm 146 James 2.1–10 [11–13] 14–17 Mark 7.24–end	Psalm 119.57–72 Jonah 3.10—4.11 *or* Ecclesiasticus 27.30—28.9 Revelation 8.1–5	Psalm 119.41–56 [*or* 119.49–56] Exodus 14.5–end Matthew 6.1–18

			Holy Communion	Morning Prayer	Evening Prayer
Monday	**10 September** DEL week 23	*G*	1 Corinthians 5.1–8 Psalm 5.5–9*a* Luke 6.6–11	Psalms 27, **30** 1 Kings 8.31–62 Acts 16.6–24	Psalms 26, **28**, 29 Zechariah 10 Mark 11.1–11
Tuesday	**11 September**	*G*	1 Corinthians 6.1–11 Psalm 149.1–5 Luke 6.12–19	Psalms 32, **36** 1 Kings 8.63—9.9 Acts 16.25–end	Psalm **33** Zechariah 11.4–end Mark 11.12–26
Wednesday	**12 September**	*G*	1 Corinthians 7.25–31 Psalm 45.11–end Luke 6.20–26	Psalm **34** 1 Kings 10.1–25 Acts 17.1–15	Psalm **119.33–56** Zechariah 12.1–10 Mark 11.27–end
Thursday	**13 September** John Chrysostom, bishop, teacher of the faith, 407 (see p.82)	*Gw*	1 Corinthians 8.1–7, 11–end Psalm 139.1–9 Luke 6.27–38	Psalm **37*** 1 Kings 11.1–13 Acts 17.16–end	Psalms 39, **40** Zechariah 13 Mark 12.1–12 *or:* 1st EP of Holy Cross Day: Psalm 66 Isaiah 52.13—end of 53 Ephesians 2.11–end

			Principal Service	3rd Service	2nd Service
Friday	**14 September** Holy Cross Day	*R*	Numbers 21.4–9 Psalm 22.23–28 Philippians 2.6–11 John 3.13–17	*MP* Psalms 2, 8, 146 Genesis 3.1–15 John 12.27–36*a*	*EP* Psalms 110, 150 Isaiah 63.1–16 1 Corinthians 1.18–25

			Holy Communion	Morning Prayer	Evening Prayer
Saturday	**15 September** Cyprian, bishop, martyr, 258 (see p.81)	*Gr*	1 Corinthians 10.14–22 Psalm 116.10–end Luke 6.43–end	Psalms 41, **42**, 43 1 Kings 12.1–24 Acts 18.22—19.7	Psalms 45, **46** Zechariah 14.12–end Mark 12.18–27

		Principal Service	3rd Service	2nd Service
Sunday	**16 September** *G* **16th Sunday after Trinity** Proper 19	*Continuous:* Proverbs 1.20–33 Psalm 19 [*or* 19.1–6] *or* *Canticle*: Wisdom 7.26—8.1 *Related:* Isaiah 50.4–9*a* Psalm 116.1–8 James 3.1–12 Mark 8.27–end	Psalm 119.105–120 Isaiah 44.24—45.8 Revelation 12.1–12	Psalm 119.73–88 [*or* 119.73–80] Exodus 18.13–26 Matthew 7.1–14
		Holy Communion	**Morning Prayer**	**Evening Prayer**
Monday	**17 September** *Gw* Hildegard, abbess, visionary, 1179 (see p.84) DEL week 24	1 Corinthians 11.17–26, 33 Psalm 40.7–11 Luke 7.1–10	Psalm **44** 1 Kings 12.25—13.10 Acts 19.8–20	Psalms **47**, 49 Ecclesiasticus 1.1–10 *or* Ezekiel 1.1–14 Mark 12.28–34
Tuesday	**18 September** *G*	1 Corinthians 12.12–14, 27–end Psalm 100 Luke 7.11–17	Psalms **48**, 52 1 Kings 13.11–end Acts 19.21–end	Psalm **50** Ecclesiasticus 1.11–end *or* Ezekiel 1.15—2.2 Mark 12.35–end
Wednesday	**19 September** *G* *Theodore, archbishop, 690*	1 Corinthians 12.31*b*—end of 13 Psalm 33.1–12 Luke 7.31–35	Psalm **119.57–80** 1 Kings 17 Acts 20.1–16	Psalms **59**, 60 (67) Ecclesiasticus 2 *or* Ezekiel 2.3—3.11 Mark 13.1–13
Thursday	**20 September** *Gr* John Coleridge Patteson, bishop, and companions, martyrs, 1871 (see p.81)	1 Corinthians 15.1–11 Psalm 118.1–2, 17–20 Luke 7.36–end	Psalms 56, **57** (63*) 1 Kings 18.1–20 Acts 20.17–end	Psalms 61, **62**, 64 Ecclesiasticus 3.17–29 *or* Ezekiel 3.12–end Mark 13.14–23 *or:* 1st EP of Matthew, Apostle and Evangelist: Psalm 34; Isaiah 33.13–17; Matthew 6.19–end
		Principal Service	**3rd Service**	**2nd Service**
Friday	**21 September** *R* Matthew, Apostle and Evangelist	Proverbs 3.13–18 Psalm 119.65–72 2 Corinthians 4.1–6 Matthew 9.9–13	*MP* Psalms 49, 117 1 Kings 19.15–end 2 Timothy 3.14–end	*EP* Psalm 119.33–40, 89–96 Ecclesiastes 5.4–12 Matthew 19.16–end
		Holy Communion	**Morning Prayer**	**Evening Prayer**
Saturday	**22 September** *G*	1 Corinthians 15.35–37, 42–49 Psalm 30.1–5 Luke 8.4–15	Psalm **68** 1 Kings 19 Acts 21.17–36	Psalms 65, **66** Ecclesiasticus 4.29—6.1 *or* Ezekiel 9 Mark 13.32–end

Day	Date	Colour	Principal Service	3rd Service	2nd Service
Sunday	**23 September** **17th Sunday after Trinity** Proper 20	*G*	*Continuous:* Proverbs 31.10–end Psalm 1 *Related:* Wisdom 1.16—2.1, 12–22 *or* Jeremiah 11.18–20 Psalm 54 James 3.13—4.3, 7–8*a* Mark 9.30–37	Psalm 119.153–end Isaiah 45.9–22 Revelation 14.1–5	Psalm 119.137–152 [*or* 119.137–144] Exodus 19.10–end Matthew 8.23–end
			Holy Communion	**Morning Prayer**	**Evening Prayer**
Monday	**24 September** DEL week 25	*G*	Proverbs 3.27–34 Psalm 15 Luke 8.16–18	Psalm **71** 1 Kings 21 Acts 21.37—22.21	Psalms **72**, 75 Ecclesiasticus 6.14–end *or* Ezekiel 10.1–19 Mark 14.1–11
Tuesday	**25 September** Lancelot Andrewes, bishop, spiritual writer, 1626 (see p.83) *Sergei of Radonezh, monastic reformer, teacher of the faith, 1392*	*Gw*	Proverbs 21.1–6, 10–13 Psalm 119.1–8 Luke 8.19–21	Psalm **73** 1 Kings 22.1–28 Acts 22.22—23.11	Psalm **74** Ecclesiasticus 7.27–end *or* Ezekiel 11.14–end Mark 14.12–25
Wednesday	**26 September** *Wilson Carlile, founder of the Church Army, 1942* Ember Day	*G*	Proverbs 30.5–9 Psalm 119.105–112 Luke 9.1–6	Psalm **77** 1 Kings 22.29–45 Acts 23.12–end	Psalm **119.81–104** Ecclesiasticus 10.6–8, 12–24 *or* Ezekiel 12.1–16 Mark 14.26–42
Thursday	**27 September** Vincent de Paul, founder of the Lazarists, 1660 (see p.84)	*Gw*	Ecclesiastes 1.2–11 Psalm 90.1–6 Luke 9.7–9	Psalm **78.1–39*** 2 Kings 1.2–17 Acts 24.1–23	Psalm **78.40–end*** Ecclesiasticus 11.7–28 *or* Ezekiel 12.17–end Mark 14.43–52
Friday	**28 September** Ember Day	*G*	Ecclesiastes 3.1–11 Psalm 144.1–4 Luke 9.18–22	Psalm **55** 2 Kings 2.1–18 Acts 24.24—25.12	Psalm **69** Ecclesiasticus 14.20—15.10 *or* Ezekiel 13.1–16 Mark 14.53–65 *or:* 1st EP of Michael and All Angels: Psalm 91; 2 Kings 6.8–17; Matthew 18.1–6, 10
			Principal Service	**3rd Service**	**2nd Service**
Saturday	**29 September** Michael and All Angels Ember Day	*W*	Genesis 28.10–17 *or* Revelation 12.7–12 Psalm 103.19–end Revelation 12.7–12 *or* Hebrews 1.5–end John 1.47–end	*MP* Psalms 34, 150 Tobit 12.6–end *or* Daniel 12.1–4 Acts 12.1–11	*EP* Psalms 138, 148 Daniel 10.4–end Revelation 5

Day	Date	Colour	Principal Service		3rd Service	2nd Service
			Continuous:	*Related:*		
Sunday	**30 September** **18th Sunday after Trinity** Proper 21	*G*	Esther 7.1–6, 9–10; 9.20–22 Psalm 124	Numbers 11.4–6, 10–16, 24–29 Psalm 19.7–end	Psalm 122 Isaiah 48.12–end Luke 11.37–end	Psalms 120, 121 Exodus 24 Matthew 9.1–8
			James 5.13–end Mark 9.38–end			

Day	Date	Colour	Holy Communion	Morning Prayer	Evening Prayer
Monday	**1 October** *Remigius, bishop, 533* *Anthony Ashley Cooper (Earl of Shaftesbury), social reformer, 1885* DEL week 26	*G*	Job 1.6–end Psalm 17.1–11 Luke 9.46–50	Psalms **80**, 82 2 Kings 5 Acts 26.1–23	Psalms **85**, 86 Ecclesiasticus 16.17–end *or* Ezekiel 14.12–end Mark 15.1–15
Tuesday	**2 October**	*G*	Job 3.1–3, 11–17, 20–23 Psalm 88.14–19 Luke 9.51–56	Psalms 87, **89.1–18** 2 Kings 6.1–23 Acts 26.24–end	Psalm **89.19–end** Ecclesiasticus 17.1–24 *or* Ezekiel 18.1–20 Mark 15.16–32
Wednesday	**3 October** *George Bell, bishop, ecumenist, peacemaker, 1958*	*G*	Job 9.1–12, 14–16 Psalm 88.1–6, 11 Luke 9.57–end	Psalm **119.105–128** 2 Kings 9.1–16 Acts 27.1–26	Psalms **91**, 93 Ecclesiasticus 18.1–14 *or* Ezekiel 18.21–32 Mark 15.33–41
Thursday	**4 October** Francis of Assisi, friar, deacon, 1226 (see p.84)	*Gw*	Job 19.21–27*a* Psalm 27.13–16 Luke 10.1–12	Psalms 90, **92** 2 Kings 9.17–end Acts 27.27–end	Psalm **94** Ecclesiasticus 19.4–17 *or* Ezekiel 20.1–20 Mark 15.42–end
Friday	**5 October**	*G*	Job 38.1, 12–21; 40.3–5 Psalm 139.6–11 Luke 10.13–16	Psalms **88** (95) 2 Kings 12.1–19 Acts 28.1–16	Psalm **102** Ecclesiasticus 19.20–end *or* Ezekiel 20.21–38 Mark 16.1–8
Saturday	**6 October** William Tyndale, translator, martyr, 1536 (see p.81)	*Gr*	Job 42.1–3, 6, 12–end Psalm 119.169–end Luke 10.17–24	Psalms 96, **97**, 100 2 Kings 17.1–23 Acts 28.17–end	Psalm **104** Ecclesiasticus 21.1–17 *or* Ezekiel 24.15–end Mark 16.9–end

		Principal Service	3rd Service	2nd Service
Sunday	**7 October** *G* **19th Sunday after Trinity** Proper 22	*Continuous:* Job 1.1; 2.1–10 Psalm 26 *Related:* Genesis 2.18–24 Psalm 8 Hebrews 1.1–4; 2.5–12 Mark 10.2–16	Psalms 123, 124 Isaiah 49.13–23 Luke 12.1–12	Psalms 125, 126 Joshua 3.7–end Matthew 10.1–22
		Holy Communion	Morning Prayer	Evening Prayer
Monday	**8 October** *G* DEL week 27	Galatians 1.6–12 Psalm 111.1–6 Luke 10.25–37	Psalms **98**, 99, 101 2 Kings 17.24–end Philippians 1.1–11	Psalm **105*** (*or* 103) Ecclesiasticus 22.6–22 *or* Ezekiel 28.1–19 John 13.1–11
Tuesday	**9 October** *G* *Denys, bishop, and companions, martyrs, c.250* *Robert Grosseteste, bishop, philosopher, scientist, 1253*	Galatians 1.13–end Psalm 139.1–9 Luke 10.38–end	Psalm **106*** (*or* 103) 2 Kings 18.1–12 Philippians 1.12–end	Psalm **107*** Ecclesiasticus 22.27—23.15 *or* Ezekiel 33.1–20 John 13.12–20
Wednesday	**10 October** *Gw* Paulinus, bishop, missionary, 644 (see p.84) *Thomas Traherne, poet, spiritual writer, 1674*	Galatians 2.1–2, 7–14 Psalm 117 Luke 11.1–4	Psalms 110, **111**, 112 2 Kings 18.13–end Philippians 2.1–13	Psalm **119.129–152** Ecclesiasticus 24.1–22 *or* Ezekiel 33.21–end John 13.21–30
Thursday	**11 October** *G* *Ethelburga, abbess, 675* *James the Deacon, companion of Paulinus, 7th cent.*	Galatians 3.1–5 *Canticle:* Benedictus Luke 11.5–13	Psalms 113, **115** 2 Kings 19.1–19 Philippians 2.14–end	Psalms 114, **116**, 117 Ecclesiasticus 24.23–end *or* Ezekiel 34.1–16 John 13.31–end
Friday	**12 October** *Gw* Wilfrid, bishop, missionary, 709 (see p.84) *Elizabeth Fry, prison reformer, 1845* *Edith Cavell, nurse, 1915*	Galatians 3.7–14 Psalm 111.4–end Luke 11.15–26	Psalm **139** 2 Kings 19.20–36 Philippians 3.1—4.1	Psalms **130**, 131, 137 Ecclesiasticus 27.30—28.9 *or* Ezekiel 34.17–end John 14.1–14
Saturday	**13 October** *Gw* Edward the Confessor, king, 1066 (see p.85)	Galatians 3.22–end; Psalm 105.1–7 Luke 11.27–28	Psalms 120, **121**, 122 2 Kings 20 Philippians 4.2–end	Psalm **118** Ecclesiasticus 28.14–end *or* Ezekiel 36.16–36 John 14.15–end

			Principal Service	3rd Service	2nd Service
Sunday	**14 October** **20th Sunday after Trinity** Proper 23	*G*	*Continuous:* Job 23.1–9, 16–end Psalm 22.1–15 *Related:* Amos 5.6–7, 10–15 Psalm 90.12–end Hebrews 4.12–end Mark 10.17–31	Psalms 129, 130 Isaiah 50.4–10 Luke 13.22–30	Psalms 127 [128] Joshua 5.13—6.20 Matthew 11.20–end
			Holy Communion	**Morning Prayer**	**Evening Prayer**
Monday	**15 October** Teresa of Avila, teacher of the faith, 1582 (see p.82) DEL week 28	*Gw*	Galatians 4.21–24, 26–27, 31; 5.1 Psalm 113 Luke 11.29–32	Psalms 123, 124, 125, **126** 2 Kings 21.1–18 1 Timothy 1.1–17	Psalms **127**, 128, 129 Ecclesiasticus 31.1–11 *or* Ezekiel 37.1–14 John 15.1–11
Tuesday	**16 October** *Nicholas Ridley and Hugh Latimer, bishops, martyrs, 1555*	*G*	Galatians 5.1–6 Psalm 119.41–48 Luke 11.37–41	Psalms **132**, 133 2 Kings 22.1—23.3 1 Timothy 1.18—end of 2	Psalms (134,) **135** Ecclesiasticus 34.9–end *or* Ezekiel 37.15–end John 15.12–17
Wednesday	**17 October** Ignatius, bishop, martyr, c.107 (see p.81)	*Gr*	Galatians 5.18–end Psalm 1 Luke 11.42–46	Psalm **119.153–end** 2 Kings 23.4–25 1 Timothy 3	Psalm **136** Ecclesiasticus 35 *or* Ezekiel 39.21–end John 15.18–end *or:* 1st EP of Luke the Evangelist: Psalm 33; Hosea 6.1–3; 2 Timothy 3.10–end
			Principal Service	**3rd Service**	**2nd Service**
Thursday	**18 October** Luke the Evangelist	*R*	Isaiah 35.3–6 *or* Acts 16.6–12*a* Psalm 147.1–7 2 Timothy 4.5–17 Luke 10.1–9	*MP* Psalms 145, 146 Isaiah 55 Luke 1.1–4	*EP* Psalm 103 Ecclesiasticus 38.1–14 *or* Isaiah 61.1–6 Colossians 4.7–end
			Holy Communion	**Morning Prayer**	**Evening Prayer**
Friday	**19 October** Henry Martyn, translator, missionary, 1812 (see p.84)	*Gw*	Ephesians 1.11–14 Psalm 33.1–6, 12 Luke 12.1–7	Psalms 142, **144** 2 Kings 24.18—25.12 1 Timothy 5.1–16	Psalm **145** Ecclesiasticus 38.1–14 *or* Ezekiel 44.4–16 John 16.16–22
Saturday	**20 October**	*G*	Ephesians 1.15–end Psalm 8 Luke 12.8–12	Psalm **147** 2 Kings 25.22–end 1 Timothy 5.17–end	Psalms **148**, 149, 150 Ecclesiasticus 38.24–end *or* Ezekiel 47.1–12 John 16.23–end

Day	Date		Principal Service	3rd Service	2nd Service
Sunday	**21 October** **21st Sunday after Trinity** Proper 24	*G*	*Continuous:* Job 38.1–7 [34–end] Psalm 104.1–10, 26, 35c [*or* 104.1–10] *Related:* Isaiah 53.4–end Psalm 91.9–end Hebrews 5.1–10 Mark 10.35–45	Psalms 133, 134, 137.1–6 Isaiah 54.1–14 Luke 13.31–end	Psalms 141 Joshua 14.6–14 Matthew 12.1–21
			Holy Communion	**Morning Prayer**	**Evening Prayer**
Monday	**22 October** DEL week 29	*G*	Ephesians 2.1–10 Psalm 100 Luke 12.13–21	Psalms **1**, 2, 3 Judith 4 *or* Exodus 22.21–27; 23.1–17 1 Timothy 6.1–10	Psalms **4**, 7 Ecclesiasticus 39.1–11 *or* Ecclesiastes 1 John 17.1–5
Tuesday	**23 October**	*G*	Ephesians 2.12–end Psalm 85.7–end Luke 12.35–38	Psalms **5**, 6 (8) Judith 5.1—6.4 *or* Exodus 29.38—30.16 1 Timothy 6.11–end	Psalms **9**, 10* Ecclesiasticus 39.13–end *or* Ecclesiastes 2 John 17.6–19
Wednesday	**24 October**	*G*	Ephesians 3.2–12 Psalm 98 Luke 12.39–48	Psalm **119.1–32** Judith 6.10—7.7 *or* Leviticus 8 2 Timothy 1.1–14	Psalms **11**, 12, 13 Ecclesiasticus 42.15–end *or* Ecclesiastes 3.1–15 John 17.20–end
Thursday	**25 October** *Crispin and Crispinian, martyrs, c.287*	*G*	Ephesians 3.14–end Psalm 33.1–6 Luke 12.49–53	Psalms 14, **15**, 16 Judith 7.19–end *or* Leviticus 9 2 Timothy 1.15—2.13	Psalm **18*** Ecclesiasticus 43.1–12 *or* Ecclesiastes 3.16—end of 4 John 18.1–11
Friday	**26 October** Alfred, king, scholar, 899 (see p.85) *Cedd, abbot, bishop, 664*	*Gw*	Ephesians 4.1–6 Psalm 24.1–6 Luke 12.54–end	Psalms 17, **19** Judith 8.9–end *or* Leviticus 16.2–24 2 Timothy 2.14–end	Psalm **22** Ecclesiasticus 43.13–end *or* Ecclesiastes 5 John 18.12–27
Saturday	**27 October**	*G*	Ephesians 4.7–16 Psalm 122 Luke 13.1–9	Psalms 20, 21, **23** Judith 9 *or* Leviticus 17 2 Timothy 3	Psalms **24**, 25 Ecclesiasticus 44.1–15 *or* Ecclesiastes 6 John 18.28–end *or:* 1st EP of Simon and Jude, Apostles: Psalms 124, 125, 126 Deuteronomy 32.1–4 John 14.15–26

Simon and Jude / Last after Trinity

If Simon and Jude, Apostles *is celebrated on Sunday 28 October:*

		Principal Service	3rd Service	2nd Service
Sunday	**28 October** *R* Simon and Jude, Apostles	Isaiah 28.14–16 Psalm 119.89–96 Ephesians 2.19–end John 15.17–end	*MP* Psalms 116, 117 Wisdom 5.1–16 *or* Isaiah 45.18–end Luke 6.12–16	*EP* Psalm 119.1–16 1 Maccabees 2.42–66 *or* Jeremiah 3.11–18 Jude 1–4, 17–end
		Holy Communion	**Morning Prayer**	**Evening Prayer**
Monday	**29 October** *Gr* James Hannington, bishop, martyr, 1885 (see p.81) DEL week 30	Ephesians 4.32—5.8 Psalm 1 Luke 13.10–17	Psalms 27, **30** Judith 10 *or* Leviticus 19.1–18, 30–end 2 Timothy 4.1–8	Psalms 26, **28**, 29 Ecclesiasticus 44.19—45.5 *or* Ecclesiastes 7.1–14 John 19.1–16

If Simon and Jude, Apostles *is transferred to Monday 29 October:*

		Principal Service	3rd Service	2nd Service
Sunday	**28 October** *G* **Last Sunday after Trinity** Proper 25	*Continuous:* Job 42.1–6, 10–end Psalm 34.1–8, 19–end [*or* 34.1–8] *Related:* Jeremiah 31.7–9 Psalm 126 Hebrews 7.23–end Mark 10.46–end	Psalm 119.89–104 Isaiah 59.9–20 Luke 14.1–14	Psalm 119.121–136 Ecclesiastes 11, 12 2 Timothy 2.1–7 *HC* Luke 18.9–14 *or:* 1st EP of Simon and Jude, Apostles: Psalms 124, 125, 126 Deuteronomy 32.1–4 John 14.15–26
or **Sunday**	**28 October** *G* **Bible Sunday**	Isaiah 55.1–11 Psalm 19.7–end 2 Timothy 3.14—4.5 John 5.36*b*–end	Psalm 119.89–104 Isaiah 45.22–end Matthew 24.30–35 *or* Luke 14.1–14	Psalm 119.1–16 2 Kings 22 Colossians 3.12–17 *HC* Luke 4.14–30 *or:* 1st EP of Simon and Jude, Apostles: Psalms 124, 125, 126 Deuteronomy 32.1–4 John 14.15–26

or, if the date of dedication of a church is not known, the Dedication Festival *(Gold or W) may be celebrated today or on 7 October, or on a suitable date chosen locally* *(see p.80)*

		Principal Service	3rd Service	2nd Service
Monday	**29 October** *R* Simon and Jude, Apostles *(transferred from 28 October)*	Isaiah 28.14–16 Psalm 119.89–96 Ephesians 2.19–end John 15.17–end	*MP* Psalms 116, 117 Wisdom 5.1–16 *or* Isaiah 45.18–end Luke 6.12–16	*EP* Psalm 119.1–16 1 Maccabees 2.42–66 *or* Jeremiah 3.11–18 Jude 1–4, 17–end

			Holy Communion	Morning Prayer	Evening Prayer
Tuesday	**30 October** DEL week 30	*G*	Ephesians 5.21–end Psalm 128 Luke 13.18–21	Psalms 32, **36** Judith 11 *or* Leviticus 23.1–22 2 Timothy 4.9–end	Psalm **33** Ecclesiasticus 45.6–17 *or* Ecclesiastes 7.15–end John 19.17–30
Wednesday	**31 October** *Martin Luther, reformer, 1546*	*G*	Ephesians 6.1–9 Psalm 145.10–20 Luke 13.22–30	Psalm **34** Judith 12 *or* Leviticus 23.23–end Titus 1	Psalm **119.33–56** Ecclesiasticus 46.1–10 *or* Ecclesiastes 8 John 19.31–end *or, if All Saints' Day is celebrated on Thursday 1 November only:* **1st EP of All Saints' Day:** Psalms 1, 5 Ecclesiasticus 44.1–15 *or* Isaiah 40.27–end Revelation 19.6–10

All Saints' Day / 4 before Advent

All Saints' Day is celebrated either on Thursday 1 November or on Sunday 4 November; if the latter there may be a supplementary celebration on 1 November.

			Principal Service	3rd Service	2nd Service
	If All Saints' Day is celebrated on Thursday 1 November only:				
Thursday	**1 November** **All Saints' Day**	*Gold or W*	Wisdom 3.1–9 *or* Isaiah 25.6–9 Psalm 24.1–6 Revelation 21.1–6*a* John 11.32–44	*MP* Psalms 15, 84, 149 Isaiah 35.1–9 Luke 9.18–27	*EP* Psalms 148, 150 Isaiah 65.17–end Hebrews 11.32—12.2
			Principal Service	**3rd Service**	**2nd Service**
	If All Saints' Day is celebrated on Thursday 1 November in addition to Sunday 4 November:				
Thursday	**1 November** **All Saints' Day**	*Gold or W*	Isaiah 56.3–8 *or* 2 Esdras 2.42–end Psalm 33.1–5 Hebrews 12.18–24 Matthew 5.1–12	*MP* Psalms 111, 112, 117 Wisdom 5.1–16 *or* Jeremiah 31.31–34 2 Corinthians 4.5–12	*EP* Psalm 145 Isaiah 66.20–23 Colossians 1.9–14
			Holy Communion	**Morning Prayer**	**Evening Prayer**
Friday	**2 November** Commemoration of the Faithful Departed (All Souls' Day)	*Rp/Gp*	Philippians 1.1–11 Psalm 111 Luke 14.1–6 *Lesser Festival eucharistic lectionary:* Lamentations 3.17–26, 31–33 *or* Wisdom 3.1–9 Psalm 23 *or* 27.1–6,16–17 Romans 5.5–11 *or* 1 Peter 1.3–9 John 5.19–25 *or* John 6.37–40	Psalm **31** Judith 15.1–13 *or* Leviticus 25.1–24 Titus 3	Psalm **35** Ecclesiasticus 51.1–12 *or* Ecclesiastes 11.1–8 John 20.11–18
Saturday	**3 November** Richard Hooker, priest, teacher of the faith, 1600 (p. 82) *Martin of Porres, friar, 1639*	*Rw/Gw*	Philippians 1.18–26 Psalm 42.1–7 Luke 14.1, 7–11	Psalms 41, **42**, 43 Judith 15.14—end of 16 *or* Numbers 6.1–5, 21–end Philemon	Psalms 45, **46** Ecclesiasticus 51.13–end *or* Ecclesiastes 11.9—end of 12 John 20.19–end
			Principal Service	**3rd Service**	**2nd Service**
Sunday	**4 November** **4th Sunday before Advent**	*R/G*	Deuteronomy 6.1–9 Psalm 119.1–8 Hebrews 9.11–14 Mark 12.28–34	Psalms 112, 149 Jeremiah 31.31–34 1 John 3.1–3	Psalm 145 [*or* 145.1–9] Daniel 2.1–48 (*or* 1–11, 25–48) Revelation 7.9–end *HC* Matthew 5.1–12

			Holy Communion	Morning Prayer	Evening Prayer
	If All Saints' Day is celebrated on Sunday 4 November only:				
Thursday	**1 November**	*G*	Ephesians 6.10–20 Psalm 144.1–2, 9–11 Luke 13.31–end	Psalm **37*** Judith 13 *or* Leviticus 24.1–9 Titus 2	Psalms 39, **40** Ecclesiasticus 50.1–24 *or* Ecclesiastes 9 John 20.1–10
Friday	**2 November** Commemoration of the Faithful Departed (All Souls' Day)	*Gp*	Philippians 1.1–11 Psalm 111 Luke 14.1–6 *Lesser Festival eucharistic lectionary:* Lamentations 3.17–26, 31–33 *or* Wisdom 3.1–9 Psalm 23 *or* 27.1–6,16–17 Romans 5.5–11 *or* 1 Peter 1.3–9 John 5.19–25 *or* John 6.37–40	Psalm **31** Judith 15.1–13 *or* Leviticus 25.1–24 Titus 3	Psalm **35** Ecclesiasticus 51.1–12 *or* Ecclesiastes 11.1–8 John 20.11–18
Saturday	**3 November** Richard Hooker, priest, teacher of the faith, 1600 (p. 82) *Martin of Porres, friar, 1639*	*Gw*	Philippians 1.18–26 Psalm 42.1–7 Luke 14.1, 7–11	Psalms 41, **42**, 43 Judith 15.14—end of 16 *or* Numbers 6.1–5, 21–end Philemon	Psalms 45, **46** Ecclesiasticus 51.13–end *or* Ecclesiastes 11.9–end of 12 John 20.19–end *or, if All Saints' Day is celebrated on Sunday 4 November:* **1st EP of All Saints' Day:** Psalms 1, 5 Ecclesiasticus 44.1–15 *or* Isaiah 40.27–end Revelation 19.6–10
			Principal Service	**3rd Service**	**2nd Service**
Sunday	**4 November** **All Saints' Day**	*Gold or W*	Wisdom 3.1–9 *or* Isaiah 25.6–9 Psalm 24.1–6 Revelation 21.1–6*a* John 11.32–44	*MP* Psalms 15, 84, 149 Isaiah 35.1–9 Luke 9.18–27	*EP* Psalms 148, 150 Isaiah 65.17–end Hebrews 11.32—12.2

		Holy Communion	Morning Prayer	Evening Prayer
Monday	**5 November** *R/G* DEL week 31	Philippians 2.1–4 Psalm 131 Luke 14.12–14	Psalms **2**, 146 *or* **44** Daniel 1 Revelation 1	Psalm **92**, 96, 97 *or* **47**, 49 Isaiah 1.1–20 Matthew 1.18–end
Tuesday	**6 November** *R/G* *Leonard, hermit, 6th cent.* *William Temple, archbishop, teacher of the faith, 1944*	Philippians 2.5–11 Psalm 22.22–27 Luke 14.15–24	Psalms **5**, 147.1–12 *or* **48**, 52 Daniel 2.1–24 Revelation 2.1–11	Psalms 98. 99, **100** *or* **50** Isaiah 1.21–end Matthew 2.1–15
Wednesday	**7 November** *Rw/Gw* Willibrord, bishop, 739 (see p.84)	Philippians 2.12–18 Psalm 27.1–5 Luke 14.25–33	Psalms **9**, 147.13–end *or* **119.57–80** Daniel 2.25–end Revelation 2.12–end	Psalm 111, **112**, 116 *or* **59**, 60 (67) Isaiah 2.1–11 Matthew 2.16–end
Thursday	**8 November** *Rw/Gw* Saints and Martyrs of England	Philippians 3.3–8*a* Psalm 105.1–7 Luke 15.1–10 *Lesser Festival eucharistic lectionary:* Isaiah 61.4–9 *or* Ecclesiasticus 44.1–15 Psalm 15 Revelation 19.5–10 John 17.18–23	Psalms 11, **15**, 148 *or* 56, **57** (63*) Daniel 3.1–18 Revelation 3.1–13	Psalm **118** *or* 61, **62**, 64 Isaiah 2.12–end Matthew 3
Friday	**9 November** *R/G* *Margery Kempe, mystic, c.1440*	Philippians 3.17—4.1 Psalm 122 Luke 16.1–8	Psalms **16**, 149 *or* **51**, 54 Daniel 3.19–end Revelation 3.14–end	Psalms 137, 138, **143** *or* **38** Isaiah 3.1–15 Matthew 4.1–11
Saturday	**10 November** *Rw/Gw* Leo the Great, bishop, teacher of the faith, 461 (see p.82)	Philippians 4.10–19 Psalm 112 Luke 16.9–15	Psalms **18.31–end**, 150 *or* **68** Daniel 4.1–18 Revelation 4	Psalm **145** *or* 65, **66** Isaiah 4.2—5.7 Matthew 4.12–22

		Principal Service	3rd Service	2nd Service
Sunday	**11 November** *R/G* **3rd Sunday before Advent** *Remembrance Sunday*	Jonah 3.1–5, 10 Psalm 62.5–end Hebrews 9.24–end Mark 1.14–20	Psalm 136 Micah 4.1–5 Philippians 4.6–9	Psalms 46 [82] Isaiah 10.33—11.9 John 14.1–29 (*or* 23–29)
		Holy Communion	**Morning Prayer**	**Evening Prayer**
Monday	**12 November** *R/G* DEL week 32	Titus 1.1–9 Psalm 24.1–6 Luke 17.1–6	Psalms 19, **20** *or* **71** Daniel 4.19–end Revelation 5	Psalm **34** *or* **72**, 75 Isaiah 5.8–24 Matthew 4.23—5.12
Tuesday	**13 November** *Rw/Gw* Charles Simeon, priest, evangelical divine, 1836 (see p.83)	Titus 2.1–8 Psalm 37.3–5, 30–32 Luke 17.7–10	Psalms **21**, 24 *or* **73** Daniel 5.1–12 Revelation 6	Psalms 36, **40** *or* **74** Isaiah 5.25–end Matthew 5.13–20
Wednesday	**14 November** *R/G* *Samuel Seabury, bishop, 1796*	Titus 3.1–7 Psalm 23 Luke 17.11–19	Psalms **23**, 25 *or* **77** Daniel 5.13–end Revelation 7.1–4, 9–end	Psalm **37** *or* **119.81–104** Isaiah 6 Matthew 5.21–37
Thursday	**15 November** *R/G*	Philemon 7–20 Psalm 146.4–end Luke 17.20–25	Psalms **26**, 27 *or* **78.1–39*** Daniel 6 Revelation 8	Psalms 42, **43** *or* **78.40–end*** Isaiah 7.1–17 Matthew 5.38–end
Friday	**16 November** *Rw/Gw* Margaret, queen, philanthropist, 1093 (see p.85) *Edmund Rich, archbishop, 1240*	2 John 4–9 Psalm 119.1–8 Luke 17.26–end	Psalms 28, **32** *or* **55** Daniel 7.1–14 Revelation 9.1–12	Psalm **31** *or* **69** Isaiah 8.1–15 Matthew 6.1–18
Saturday	**17 November** *Rw/Gw* Hugh, bishop, 1200 (see p.83)	3 John 5–8 Psalm 112 Luke 18.1–8	Psalm **33** *or* **76**, 79 Daniel 7.15–end Revelation 9.13–end	Psalms 84, **86** *or* 81, **84** Isaiah 8.16—9.7 Matthew 6.19–end

		Principal Service	3rd Service	2nd Service
Sunday	**18 November** *R/G* **2nd Sunday before Advent**	Daniel 12.1–3 Psalm 16 Hebrews 10.11–14 [15–18]19–25 Mark 13.1–8	Psalm 96 1 Samuel 9.27—10.2*a*; 10.17–26 Matthew 13.31–35	Psalm 95 Daniel 3 (*or* 3.13–end) Matthew 13.24–30, 36–43
		Holy Communion	**Morning Prayer**	**Evening Prayer**
Monday	**19 November** *Rw/Gw* Hilda, abbess, 680 (see p.84) *Mechtild, béguine, mystic, 1280* DEL week 33	Revelation 1.1–4, 2.1–5 Psalm 1 Luke 18.35–end	Psalms 46, **47** *or* **80**, 82 Daniel 8.1–14 Revelation 10	Psalms 70, **71** *or* **85**, 86 Isaiah 9.8—10.4 Matthew 7.1–12
Tuesday	**20 November** *R/Gr* Edmund, king, martyr, 870 (see p.81) *Priscilla Lydia Sellon, a restorer of the religious life in the Church of England, 1876*	Revelation 3.1–6; 14–end Psalm 15 Luke 19.1–10	Psalms 48, **52** *or* 87, **89.1–18** Daniel 8.15–end Revelation 11.1–14	Psalms **67**, 72 *or* **89.19–end** Isaiah 10.5–19 Matthew 7.13–end
Wednesday	**21 November** *R/G*	Revelation 4 Psalm 150 Luke 19.11–28	Psalms **56**, 57 *or* **119.105–128** Daniel 9.1–19 Revelation 11.15–end	Psalm **73** *or* **91**, 93 Isaiah 10.20–32 Matthew 8.1–13
Thursday	**22 November** *R/G* *Cecilia, martyr, c.230*	Revelation 5.1–10 Psalm 149.1–5 Luke 19.41–44	Psalms 61, **62** *or* 90, **92** Daniel 9.20–end Revelation 12	Psalms 74, **76** *or* **94** Isaiah 10.33—11.9 Matthew 8.14–22
Friday	**23 November** *R/Gr* Clement, bishop, martyr, c.100 (see p.81)	Revelation 10.8–end Psalm 119.65–72 Luke 19.45–end	Psalms **63**, 65 *or* **88** (95) Daniel 10.1—11.1 Revelation 13.1–10	Psalm **77** *or* **102** Isaiah 11.10—end of 12 Matthew 8.23–end
Saturday	**24 November** *R/G*	Revelation 11.4–12 Psalm 144.1–9 Luke 20.27–40	Psalms **78.1–39** *or* 96, **97**, 100 Daniel 12 Revelation 13.11–end	Psalm **78.40–end** *or* **104** Isaiah 13.1–13 Matthew 9.1–17 *or:* 1st EP of Christ the King: Psalms 99, 100 Isaiah 10.33—11.9 1 Timothy 6.11–16

			Principal Service	3rd Service	2nd Service
Sunday	**25 November** Christ the King *Sunday next before Advent*	*R/W*	Daniel 7.9–10, 13–14 Psalm 93 Revelation 1.4*b*–8 John 18.33–37	*MP* Psalms 29, 110 Isaiah 32.1–8 Revelation 3.7–end	*EP* Psalm 72 [*or* 72.1–7] Daniel 5 John 6.1–15
			Holy Communion	**Morning Prayer**	**Evening Prayer**
Monday	**26 November** DEL week 34	*R/G*	Revelation 14.1–5 Psalm 24.1–6 Luke 21.1–4	Psalms 92, **96** *or* **98**, 99, 101 Isaiah 40.1–11 Revelation 14.1–13	Psalms **80**, 81 *or* **105*** (*or* 103) Isaiah 14.3–20 Matthew 9.18–34
Tuesday	**27 November**	*R/G*	Revelation 14.14–19 Psalm 96 Luke 21.5–11	Psalms **97**, 98, 100 *or* **106*** (*or* 103) Isaiah 40.12–26 Revelation 14.14—end of 15	Psalms 99, **101** *or* **107*** Isaiah 17 Matthew 9.35—10.15
Wednesday	**28 November**	*R/G*	Revelation 15.1–4 Psalm 98 Luke 21.12–19	Psalms 110, 111, **112** *or* 110, **111**, 112 Isaiah 40.27—41.7 Revelation 16.1–11	Psalms 121, **122**, 123, 124 *or* **119.129–152** Isaiah 19 Matthew 10.16–33
Thursday	**29 November** *Day of Intercession and Thanksgiving for the Missionary Work of the Church*	*R/G*	Revelation 18.1–2, 21–23, 19.1–3, 9 Psalm 100 Luke 21.20–28	Psalms **125**, 126, 127, 128 *or* 113, **115** Isaiah 41.8–20 Revelation 16.12–end	Psalms 131, 132, **133** *or* 114, **116**, 117 Isaiah 21.1–12 Matthew 10.34—11.1 *or:* 1st EP of Andrew the Apostle: Psalm 48 Isaiah 49.1–9*a* 1 Corinthians 4.9–16
			Principal Service	**3rd Service**	**2nd Service**
Friday	**30 November** Andrew the Apostle	*R*	Isaiah 52.7–10 Psalm 19.1–6 Romans 10.12–18 Matthew 4.18–22	*MP* Psalms 47, 147.1–12 Ezekiel 47.1–12 *or* Ecclesiasticus 14.20–end John 12.20–32	*EP* Psalms 87, 96 Zechariah 8.20–end John 1.35–42
			Holy Communion	**Morning Prayer**	**Evening Prayer**
Saturday	**1 December** *Charles de Foucauld, hermit, 1916*	*R/G*	Revelation 22.1–7 Psalm 95.1–7 Luke 21.34–36	Psalm **145** *or* 120, **121**, 122 Isaiah 42.10–17 Revelation 18	Psalms 148, 149, **150** *or* **118** Isaiah 24 Matthew 11.20–end

¶ *Additional Weekday Lectionary*

This Additional Weekday Lectionary provides two readings for each day of the year, except for Sundays, Principal Feasts and other Principal Holy Days, Holy Week and Festivals (for which the readings provided in the main body of this lectionary are used). The readings for 'first evensongs' in the main body of the lectionary are used on the eves of Principal Feasts and may be used on the eves of Festivals. This lectionary is intended particularly for use in those places of worship that attract occasional rather than daily worshippers, and can be used either at Morning or Evening Prayer. Psalmody is not provided and should be taken from the daily provision earlier in this volume.

	3 December – Advent 1		
Monday	**4 December**	Malachi 3.1–6	Matthew 3.1–6
Tuesday	**5 December**	Zephaniah 3.14–end	1 Thessalonians 4.13–end
Wednesday	**6 December**	Isaiah 65.17—66.2	Matthew 24.1–14
Thursday	**7 December**	Micah 5.2–5*a*	John 3.16–21
Friday	**8 December**	Isaiah 66.18–end	Luke 13.22–30
Saturday	**9 December**	Micah 7.8–15	Romans 15.30—16.7, 25–end
	10 December – Advent 2		
Monday	**11 December**	Jeremiah 7.1–11	Philippians 4.4–9
Tuesday	**12 December**	Daniel 7.9–14	Matthew 24.15–28
Wednesday	**13 December**	Amos 9.11–end	Romans 13.8–14
Thursday	**14 December**	Jeremiah 23.5–8	Mark 11.1–11
Friday	**15 December**	Jeremiah 33.14–22	Luke 21.25–36
Saturday	**16 December**	Zechariah 14.4–11	Revelation 22.1–7
	17 December – Advent 3		
Monday	**18 December**	Exodus 3.1–6	Acts 7.20–36
Tuesday	**19 December**	Isaiah 11.1–9	Romans 15.7–13
Wednesday	**20 December**	Isaiah 22.21–23	Revelation 3.7–13
Thursday	**21 December**	Numbers 24.15*b*–19	Revelation 22.10–21
Friday	**22 December**	Jeremiah 30.7–11*a*	Acts 4.1–12
Saturday	**23 December**	Isaiah 7.10–15	Matthew 1.18–23
	24 December – Advent 4		
Monday	**25 December**	**Christmas Day** – see p.13	
Tuesday	**26 December**	Stephen, deacon, first martyr – see p.13	
Wednesday	**27 December**	John, Apostle and Evangelist – see p.13	
Thursday	**28 December**	The Holy Innocents – see p.13	
Friday	**29 December**	Micah 1.1–4; 2.12–13	Luke 2.1–7
Saturday	**30 December**	Isaiah 9.2–7	John 8.12–20
	31 December – Christmas 1		
Monday	**1 January**	Naming and Circumcision of Jesus – see p.14	
Tuesday	**2 January**	Isaiah 66.6–14	Matthew 12.46–50
Wednesday	**3 January**	Deuteronomy 6.4–15	John 10.31–end
Thursday	**4 January**	Isaiah 63.7–16	Galatians 3.23—4.7

	5 January – 8 January		
Friday	**5 January**	*If the* **Epiphany** *is celebrated on Saturday 6 January: At Evening Prayer the readings for the Eve of the Epiphany are used. At other services, the following readings are used:*	
		Isaiah 12	2 Corinthians 2.12–end
Saturday	**6 January**	**Epiphany** – see p.15	
Sunday	**7 January**	Baptism of Christ – see p.15	
Monday	**8 January**	Isaiah 41.14–20	John 1.29–34
		If, for pastoral reasons, the **Epiphany** *is celebrated on Sunday 7 January:*	
Friday	**5 January**	Isaiah 12	2 Corinthians 2.12–end
		At Evening Prayer the readings for the Eve of the Epiphany are used. At other services, the following readings are used:	
Saturday	**6 January**	Genesis 25.19–end	Ephesians 1.1–6
Sunday	**7 January**	**Epiphany** – see p.16	
Monday	**8 January**	Baptism of Christ transferred – see p.16	
	9 January – 13 January		
Tuesday	**9 January**	Exodus 17.1–7	Acts 8.26–end
Wednesday	**10 January**	Exodus 15.1–19	Colossians 2.8–15
Thursday	**11 January**	Zechariah 6.9–15	1 Peter 2.4–10
Friday	**12 January**	Isaiah 51.7–16	Galatians 6.14–18
Saturday	**13 January**	Leviticus 16.11–22	Hebrews 10.19–25
	14 January – Epiphany 2		
Monday	**15 January**	1 Kings 17.8–16	Mark 8.1–10
Tuesday	**16 January**	1 Kings 19.1–9*a*	Mark 1.9–15
Wednesday	**17 January**	1 Kings 19.9*b*–18	Mark 9.2–13
Thursday	**18 January**	Leviticus 11.1–8, 13–19, 41–45	Acts 10.9–16
Friday	**19 January**	Isaiah 49.8–13	Acts 10.34–43
Saturday	**20 January**	Genesis 35.1–15	Acts 10.44–end
	21 January – Epiphany 3		
Monday	**22 January**	Ezekiel 37.15–end	John 17.1–19
Tuesday	**23 January**	Ezekiel 20.39–44	John 17.20–end
Wednesday	**24 January**	Nehemiah 2.1–10	Romans 12.1–8
		or 1st EP of the Conversion of Paul	
Thursday	**25 January**	Conversion of Paul – see p.19	
Friday	**26 January**	Leviticus 19.9–28	Romans 15.1–7
Saturday	**27 January**	Jeremiah 33.1–11	1 Peter 5.5*b*–end
		If, for pastoral reasons, the **Presentation of Christ** *is celebrated on Sunday 28 January the readings for the Eve of the Presentation are used at Evening Prayer.*	
	28 January – Epiphany 4 / Presentation		
Monday	**29 January**	Jonah 3	2 Corinthians 5.11–21
Tuesday	**30 January**	Proverbs 4.10–end	Matthew 5.13–20
Wednesday	**31 January**	Isaiah 61.1–9	Luke 7.18–30
Thursday	**1 February**	Isaiah 52.1–12	Matthew 10.1–15
		If the **Presentation of Christ** *is celebrated on Friday 2 February the readings for the Eve of the Presentation are used at Evening Prayer.*	
Friday	**2 February**	**Presentation of Christ** – see p.20	
		or, if, for pastoral reasons, the **Presentation of Christ** *is celebrated on Sunday 28 January:*	
		Isaiah 56.1–8	Matthew 28.16–end
Saturday	**3 February**	Habakkuk 2.1–4	Revelation 14.1–7
	4 February – 2 before Lent		
Monday	**5 February**	Isaiah 61.1–9	Mark 6.1–13
Tuesday	**6 February**	Isaiah 52.1–10	Romans 10.5–21
Wednesday	**7 February**	Isaiah 52.13—53.6	Romans 15.14–21
Thursday	**8 February**	Isaiah 53.4–12	2 Corinthians 4.1–10
Friday	**9 February**	Zechariah 8.16–end	Matthew 10.1–15
Saturday	**10 February**	Jeremiah 1.4–10	Matthew 10.16–22

	11 February – Sunday next before Lent		
Monday	**12 February**	2 Kings 2.13–22	3 John
Tuesday	**13 February**	Judges 14.5–17	Revelation 10.4–11
Wednesday	**14 February**	**Ash Wednesday** – see p.23	
Thursday	**15 February**	Genesis 2.7–end	Hebrews 2.5–end
Friday	**16 February**	Genesis 4.1–12	Hebrews 4.12–end
Saturday	**17 February**	2 Kings 22.11–end	Hebrews 5.1–10
	18 February – Lent 1		
Monday	**19 February**	Genesis 6.11–end; 7.11–16	Luke 4.14–21
Tuesday	**20 February**	Deuteronomy 31.7–13	1 John 3.1–10
Wednesday	**21 February**	Genesis 11.1–9	Matthew 24.15–28
Thursday	**22 February**	Genesis 13.1–13	1 Peter 2.13–end
Friday	**23 February**	Genesis 21.1–8	Luke 9.18–27
Saturday	**24 February**	Genesis 32.22–32	2 Peter 1.10–end
	25 February – Lent 2		
Monday	**26 February**	1 Chronicles 21.1–17	1 John 2.1–8
Tuesday	**27 February**	Zechariah 3	2 Peter 2.1–10*a*
Wednesday	**28 February**	Job 1.1–22	Luke 21.34—22.6
Thursday	**1 March**	2 Chronicles 29.1–11	Mark 11.15–19
Friday	**2 March**	Exodus 19.1–9*a*	1 Peter 1.1–9
Saturday	**3 March**	Exodus 19.9*b*–19	Acts 7.44–50
	4 March – Lent 3		
Monday	**5 March**	Joshua 4.1–13	Luke 9.1–11
Tuesday	**6 March**	Exodus 15.22–27	Hebrews 10.32–end
Wednesday	**7 March**	Genesis 9.8–17	1 Peter 3.18–end
Thursday	**8 March**	Daniel 12.5–end	Mark 13.21–end
Friday	**9 March**	Numbers 20.1–13	1 Corinthians 10.23–end
Saturday	**10 March**	Isaiah 43.14–end	Hebrews 3.1–15
	11 March – Lent 4		
Monday	**12 March**	2 Kings 24.18—25.7	1 Corinthians 15.20–34
Tuesday	**13 March**	Jeremiah 13.12–19	Acts 13.26–35
Wednesday	**14 March**	Jeremiah 13.20–27	1 Peter 1.17—2.3
Thursday	**15 March**	Jeremiah 22.11–19	Luke 11.37–52
Friday	**16 March**	Jeremiah 17.1–14	Luke 6.17–26
Saturday	**17 March**	Ezra 1	2 Corinthians 1.12–19
	18 March – Lent 5		
Monday	**19 March**	Joseph of Nazareth – see p.28	
Tuesday	**20 March**	Isaiah 58.1–14	Mark 10.32–45
Wednesday	**21 March**	Job 36.1–12	John 14.1–14
Thursday	**22 March**	Jeremiah 9.17–22	Luke 13.31–35
Friday	**23 March**	Lamentations 5.1–3,19–22	John 12.20–26
Saturday	**24 March**	Job 17.6–end	John 12.27–36
	From the Monday of Holy Week until Easter Eve the seasonal lectionary is used: see *pp.29–30.*		
	1 April – Easter		
Monday	**2 April**	Isaiah 54.1–14	Romans 1.1–7
Tuesday	**3 April**	Isaiah 51.1–11	John 5.19–29
Wednesday	**4 April**	Isaiah 26.1–19	John 20.1–10
Thursday	**5 April**	Isaiah 43.14–21	Revelation 1.4–end
Friday	**6 April**	Isaiah 42.10–17	1 Thessalonians 5.1–11
Saturday	**7 April**	Job 14.1–14	John 21.1–14
	8 April – Easter 2		
Monday	**9 April**	**Annunciation of Our Lord to the Blessed Virgin Mary** transferred – see p.32	
Tuesday	**10 April**	Proverbs 8.1–11	Acts 16.6–15
Wednesday	**11 April**	Hosea 5.15—6.6	1 Corinthians 15.1–11
Thursday	**12 April**	Jonah 2	Mark 4.35–end
Friday	**13 April**	Genesis 6.9–end	1 Peter 3.8–end
Saturday	**14 April**	1 Samuel 2.1–8	Matthew 28.8–15

	15 April – Easter 3		
Monday	**16 April**	Exodus 24.1–11	Revelation 5
Tuesday	**17 April**	Leviticus 19.9–18, 32–end	Matthew 5.38–end
Wednesday	**18 April**	Genesis 3.8–21	1 Corinthians 15.12–28
Thursday	**19 April**	Isaiah 33.13–22	Mark 6.47–end
Friday	**20 April**	Nehemiah 9.6–17	Romans 5.12–end
Saturday	**21 April**	Isaiah 61.10—62.5	Luke 24.1–12
	22 April – Easter 4		
Monday	**23 April**	George, martyr, patron of England – see p.34	
Tuesday	**24 April**	Job 31.13–23 *or* 1st EP of Mark the Evangelist	Matthew 7.1–12
Wednesday	**25 April**	Mark the Evangelist – see p.34	
Thursday	**26 April**	Proverbs 28.3–end	Mark 10.17–31
Friday	**27 April**	Ecclesiastes 12.1–8	Romans 6.1–11
Saturday	**28 April**	1 Chronicles 29.10–13	Luke 24.13–35
	29 April – Easter 5		
Monday	**30 April**	Genesis 15.1–18 *or* 1st EP of Philip and James, Apostles	Romans 4.13–end
Tuesday	**1 May**	Philip and James, Apostles – see p.35	
Wednesday	**2 May**	Hosea 13.4–14	1 Corinthians 15.50–end
Thursday	**3 May**	Exodus 3.1–15	Mark 12.18–27
Friday	**4 May**	Ezekiel 36.33–end	Romans 8.1–11
Saturday	**5 May**	Isaiah 38.9–20	Luke 24.33–end
	6 May – Easter 6		
Monday	**7 May**	Proverbs 4.1–13	Philippians 2.1–11
Tuesday	**8 May**	Isaiah 32.12–end	Romans 5.1–11
Wednesday	**9 May**	*At Evening Prayer the readings for the Eve of Ascension Day are used. At other services, the following readings are used:* Isaiah 43.1–13	Titus 2.11—3.8
Thursday	**10 May**	**Ascension Day** – see p.36	
Friday	**11 May**	Exodus 35.30—36.1	Galatians 5.13–end
Saturday	**12 May**	Numbers 11.16–17, 24–29	1 Corinthians 2
	13 May – Easter 7		
Monday	**14 May**	Matthias the Apostle – see p.37	
Tuesday	**15 May**	1 Samuel 10.1–10	1 Corinthians 12.1–13
Wednesday	**16 May**	1 Kings 19.1–18	Matthew 3.13–end
Thursday	**17 May**	Ezekiel 11.14–20	Matthew 9.35—10.20
Friday	**18 May**	Ezekiel 36.22–28	Matthew 12.22–32
Saturday	**19 May**	*At Evening Prayer the readings for the Eve of Pentecost are used. At other services, the following readings are used:* Micah 3.1–8	Ephesians 6.10–20
	20 May – Pentecost		
Monday	**21 May**	Genesis 12.1–9	Romans 4.13–end
Tuesday	**22 May**	Genesis 13.1–12	Romans 12.9–end
Wednesday	**23 May**	Genesis 15	Romans 4.1–8
Thursday	**24 May**	Genesis 22.1–18	Hebrews 11.8–19
Friday	**25 May**	Isaiah 51.1–8	John 8.48–end
Saturday	**26 May**	*At Evening Prayer the readings for the Eve of Trinity Sunday are used. At other services, the following readings are used:* Ecclesiasticus 44.19–23 *or* Joshua 2.1–15	James 2.14–26

	27 May – Trinity Sunday		
Monday	**28 May**	Exodus 2.1–10	Hebrews 11.23–31
Tuesday	**29 May**	Exodus 2.11–end	Acts 7.17–29
Wednesday	**30 May**	Exodus 3.1–12 *or* 1st EP of Corpus Christi *or, where* Corpus Christi *is not celebrated as Festival:* 1st EP of the Visit of the Blessed Virgin Mary to Elizabeth	Acts 7.30–38
Thursday	**31 May**	Day of Thanksgiving for the Institution of the Holy Communion (Corpus Christi) – see p.39 *or, where* Corpus Christi *is not celebrated as a Festival:* Visit of the Blessed Virgin Mary to Elizabeth – see p.40	
Friday	**1 June**	Exodus 34.1–10 *Where* Corpus Christi *is celebrated as a Festival on 31 May:* Visit of the Blessed Virgin Mary to Elizabeth transferred – see p.39	Mark 7.1–13
Saturday	**2 June**	Exodus 34.27–end	2 Corinthians 3.7–end
	3 June – Trinity 1		
Monday	**4 June**	Genesis 37.1–11	Romans 12.9–21
Tuesday	**5 June**	Genesis 41.15–40	Mark 13.1–13
Wednesday	**6 June**	Genesis 42.17–end	Matthew 18.1–14
Thursday	**7 June**	Genesis 45.1–15	Acts 7.9–16
Friday	**8 June**	Genesis 47.1–12	1 Thessalonians 5.12–end
Saturday	**9 June**	Genesis 50.4–21	Luke 15.11–end
	10 June – Trinity 2		
Monday	**11 June**	Barnabas the Apostle – see p.42	
Tuesday	**12 June**	Proverbs 3.1–18	Matthew 5.1–12
Wednesday	**13 June**	Judges 6.1–16	Matthew 5.13–24
Thursday	**14 June**	Jeremiah 6.9–15	1 Timothy 2.1–6
Friday	**15 June**	1 Samuel 16.14–end	John 14.15–end
Saturday	**16 June**	Isaiah 6.1–9	Revelation 19.9–end
	17 June – Trinity 3		
Monday	**18 June**	Exodus 13.13*b*–end	Luke 15.1–10
Tuesday	**19 June**	Proverbs 1.20–end	James 5.13–end
Wednesday	**20 June**	Isaiah 5.8–24	James 1.17–25
Thursday	**21 June**	Isaiah 57.14–end	John 13.1–17
Friday	**22 June**	Jeremiah 15.15–end	Luke 16.19–31
Saturday	**23 June**	Isaiah 25.1–9 *or* 1st EP of Birth of John the Baptist	Acts 2.22–33
	24 June – Birth of John the Baptist / Trinity 4		
Monday	**25 June**	Exodus 20.1–17 *or* Birth of John the Baptist transferred – see p.44	Matthew 6.1–15
Tuesday	**26 June**	Proverbs 6.6–19	Luke 4.1–14
Wednesday	**27 June**	Isaiah 24.1–15	1 Corinthians 6.1–11
Thursday	**28 June**	Job 7 *or* 1st EP of Peter and Paul, Apostles (*or* Peter the Apostle)	Matthew 7 21–29
Friday	**29 June**	Peter and Paul, Apostles (*or* Peter the Apostle) – see p.45	
Saturday	**30 June**	Job 28	Hebrews 11.32—12.2
	1 July – Trinity 5		
Monday	**2 July**	Exodus 32.1–14 *or* 1st EP of Thomas the Apostle	Colossians 3.1–11
Tuesday	**3 July**	Thomas the Apostle – see p.46	
Wednesday	**4 July**	Isaiah 26.1–9	Romans 8.12–27
Thursday	**5 July**	Jeremiah 8.18—9.6	John 13.21–35
Friday	**6 July**	2 Samuel 5.1–12	Matthew 27.45–56
Saturday	**7 July**	Hosea 11.1–11	Matthew 28.1–7

	8 July – Trinity 6		
Monday	**9 July**	Exodus 40.1–16	Luke 14.15–24
Tuesday	**10 July**	Proverbs 11.1–12	Mark 12.38–44
Wednesday	**11 July**	Isaiah 33.2–10	Philippians 1.1–11
Thursday	**12 July**	Job 38	Luke 18.1–14
Friday	**13 July**	Job 42.1–6	John 3.1–15
Saturday	**14 July**	Ecclesiastes 9.1–11	Hebrews 1.1–9
	15 July – Trinity 7		
Monday	**16 July**	Numbers 23.1–12	1 Corinthians 1.10–17
Tuesday	**17 July**	Proverbs 12.1–12	Galatians 3.1–14
Wednesday	**18 July**	Isaiah 49.8–13	2 Corinthians 8.1–11
Thursday	**19 July**	Hosea 14	John 15.1–17
Friday	**20 July**	2 Samuel 18.18–end	Matthew 27.57–66
Saturday	**21 July**	Isaiah 55.1–7 *or* 1st EP of Mary Magdalene	Mark 16.1–8
	22 July – Mary Magdalene / Trinity 8		
Monday	**23 July**	Joel 3.16–21 *or* Mary Magdalene transferred – see p.49	Mark 4.21–34
Tuesday	**24 July**	Proverbs 12.13–end *or* 1st EP of James the Apostle	John 1.43–51
Wednesday	**25 July**	James the Apostle – see p.50	
Thursday	**26 July**	Isaiah 38.1–8	Mark 5.21–43
Friday	**27 July**	Jeremiah 14.1–9	Luke 8.4–15
Saturday	**28 July**	Ecclesiastes 5.10–19	1 Timothy 6.6–16
	29 July – Trinity 9		
Monday	**30 July**	Joshua 1.1–9	1 Corinthians 9.19–end
Tuesday	**31 July**	Proverbs 15.1–11	Galatians 2.15–end
Wednesday	**1 August**	Isaiah 49.1–7	1 John 1
Thursday	**2 August**	Proverbs 27.1–12	John 15.12–27
Friday	**3 August**	Isaiah 59.8–end	Mark 15.6–20
Saturday	**4 August**	Zechariah 7.8—8.8	Luke 20.27–40
	5 August – Trinity 10		
Monday	**6 August**	Transfiguration of Our Lord – see p.52	
Tuesday	**7 August**	Proverbs 15.15–end	Matthew 15.21–28
Wednesday	**8 August**	Isaiah 45.1–7	Ephesians 4.1–16
Thursday	**9 August**	Jeremiah 16.1–15	Luke 12.35–48
Friday	**10 August**	Jeremiah 18.1–11	Hebrews 1.1–9
Saturday	**11 August**	Jeremiah 26.1–19	Ephesians 3.1–13
	12 August – Trinity 11		
Monday	**13 August**	Ruth 2.1–13	Luke 10.25–37
Tuesday	**14 August**	Proverbs 16.1–11 *or* 1st EP of The Blessed Virgin Mary	Philippians 3.4*b*–end
Wednesday	**15 August**	The Blessed Virgin Mary – see p.53	
Thursday	**16 August**	Ecclesiasticus 2 *or* Ecclesiastes 2.12–25	John 16.1–15
Friday	**17 August**	Obadiah 1–10	John 19.1–16
Saturday	**18 August**	2 Kings 2.11–14	Luke 24.36–end
	19 August – Trinity 12		
Monday	**20 August**	1 Samuel 17.32–50	Matthew 8.14–22
Tuesday	**21 August**	Proverbs 17.1–15	Luke 7.1–17
Wednesday	**22 August**	Jeremiah 5.20–end	2 Peter 3.8–end
Thursday	**23 August**	Daniel 2.1–23 *or* 1st EP of Bartholomew the Apostle	Luke 10.1–20
Friday	**24 August**	Bartholomew the Apostle – see p.54	
Saturday	**25 August**	Daniel 6	Philippians 2.14–24

	26 August – Trinity 13		
Monday	**27 August**	2 Samuel 7.4–17	2 Corinthians 5.1–10
Tuesday	**28 August**	Proverbs 18.10–21	Romans 14.10–end
Wednesday	**29 August**	Judges 4.1–10	Romans 1.8–17
Thursday	**30 August**	Isaiah 49.14–end	John 16.16–24
Friday	**31 August**	Job 9.1–24	Mark 15.21–32
Saturday	**1 September**	Exodus 19.1–9	John 20.11–18
	2 September – Trinity 14		
Monday	**3 September**	Haggai 1	Mark 7.9–23
Tuesday	**4 September**	Proverbs 21.1–18	Mark 6.30–44
Wednesday	**5 September**	Hosea 11.1–11	1 John 4.9–end
Thursday	**6 September**	Lamentations 3.34–48	Romans 7.14–end
Friday	**7 September**	1 Kings 19.4–18	1 Thessalonians 3
Saturday	**8 September**	Ecclesiasticus 4.11–28 *or* Deuteronomy 29.2–15	2 Timothy 3.10–end
	9 September – Trinity 15		
Monday	**10 September**	Wisdom 6.12–21 *or* Job 12.1–16	Matthew 15.1–9
Tuesday	**11 September**	Proverbs 8.1–11	Luke 6.39–end
Wednesday	**12 September**	Proverbs 2.1–15	Colossians 1.9–20
Thursday	**13 September**	Baruch 3.14–end *or* Genesis 1.1–13 *or* 1st EP of Holy Cross Day	John 1.1–18
Friday	**14 September**	Holy Cross Day – see p.57	
Saturday	**15 September**	Wisdom 9.1–12 *or* Jeremiah 1.4–10	Luke 2.41–end
	16 September – Trinity 16		
Monday	**17 September**	Genesis 21.1–13	Luke 1.26–38
Tuesday	**18 September**	Ruth 4.7–17	Luke 2.25–38
Wednesday	**19 September**	2 Kings 4.1–7	John 2.1–11
Thursday	**20 September**	2 Kings 4.25*b*–37 *or* 1st EP of Matthew the Apostle	Mark 3.19*b*–35
Friday	**21 September**	Matthew the Apostle – see p.58	
Saturday	**22 September**	Exodus 15.19–27	Acts 1.6–14
	23 September – Trinity 17		
Monday	**24 September**	Exodus 19.16–end	Hebrews 12.18–end
Tuesday	**25 September**	1 Chronicles 16.1–13	Revelation 11.15–end
Wednesday	**26 September**	1 Chronicles 29.10–19	Colossians 3.12–17
Thursday	**27 September**	Nehemiah 8.1–12	1 Corinthians 14.1–12
Friday	**28 September**	Isaiah 1.10–17 *or* 1st EP of Michael and All Angels	Mark 12.28–34
Saturday	**29 September**	Michael and All Angels – see p.59	
	30 September – Trinity 18		
Monday	**1 October**	2 Samuel 22.4–7, 17–20	Hebrews 7.26—8.6
Tuesday	**2 October**	Proverbs 22.17–end	2 Corinthians 12.1–10
Wednesday	**3 October**	Hosea 14	James 2.14–26
Thursday	**4 October**	Isaiah 24.1–15	John 16.25–33
Friday	**5 October**	Jeremiah 14.1–9	Luke 23.44–56
Saturday	**6 October**	Zechariah 8.14–end	John 20.19–end
	7 October – Trinity 19		
Monday	**8 October**	1 Kings 3.3–14	1 Timothy 3.14—4.8
Tuesday	**9 October**	Proverbs 27.11–end	Galatians 6.1–10
Wednesday	**10 October**	Isaiah 51.1–6	2 Corinthians 1.1–11
Thursday	**11 October**	Ecclesiasticus 18.1–14 *or* Job 26	1 Corinthians 11.17–end
Friday	**12 October**	Ecclesiasticus 28.2–12 *or* Job 19.21–end	Mark 15.33–47
Saturday	**13 October**	Isaiah 44.21–end	John 21.15–end

	14 October – Trinity 20		
Monday	**15 October**	1 Kings 6.2–10	John 12.1–11
Tuesday	**16 October**	Proverbs 31.10–end	Luke 10.38–42
Wednesday	**17 October**	Jonah 1 *or* 1st EP of Luke the Evangelist	Luke 5.1–11
Thursday	**18 October**	Luke the Evangelist – see p.62	
Friday	**19 October**	Isaiah 64	Matthew 27.45–56
Saturday	**20 October**	2 Samuel 7.18–end	Acts 2.22–33
	21 October – Trinity 21		
Monday	**22 October**	1 Kings 8.22–30	John 12.12–19
Tuesday	**23 October**	Ecclesiastes 11	Luke 13.10–17
Wednesday	**24 October**	Hosea 14.1–7	2 Timothy 4.1–8
Thursday	**25 October**	Isaiah 49.1–7	John 19.16–25*a*
Friday	**26 October**	Proverbs 24.3–22	John 8.1–11
Saturday	**27 October**	Ecclesiasticus 7.8–17, 32–end *or* Deuteronomy 6.16–25 *or* 1st EP of Simon and Jude, Apostles	2 Timothy 1.1–14
	28 October – Simon and Jude / Last after Trinity		
Monday	**29 October**	Isaiah 42.14–21 *or* Simon and Jude, Apostles transferred – see p.64	Luke 1.5–25
Tuesday	**30 October**	1 Samuel 4.12–end	Luke 1.57–80
Wednesday	**31 October**	Baruch 5 *or* Haggai 1.1–11 *or* 1st EP of All Saints' Day	Mark 1.1–11
Thursday	**1 November**	**All Saints' Day** – see p.66	
Friday	**2 November**	2 Samuel 11.1–17	Matthew 14.1–12
Saturday	**3 November**	Isaiah 43.15–21 *or* 1st EP of **All Saints' Day**, *if All Saints' Day is celebrated on 4 November.*	Acts 19.1–10
	4 November – 4 before Advent / All Saints' Day		
Monday	**5 November**	Esther 3.1–11; 4.7–17	Matthew 18.1–10
Tuesday	**6 November**	Ezekiel 18.21–end	Matthew 18.12–20
Wednesday	**7 November**	Proverbs 3.27–end	Matthew 18.21–end
Thursday	**8 November**	Exodus 23.1–9	Matthew 19.1–15
Friday	**9 November**	Proverbs 3.13–18	Matthew 19.16–end
Saturday	**10 November**	Deuteronomy 28.1–6	Matthew 20.1–16
	11 November – 3 before Advent (Remembrance Sunday)		
Monday	**12 November**	Isaiah 40.21–end	Romans 11.25–end
Tuesday	**13 November**	Ezekiel 34.20–end	John 10.1–18
Wednesday	**14 November**	Leviticus 26.3–13	Titus 2.1–10
Thursday	**15 November**	Hosea 6.1–6	Matthew 9.9–13
Friday	**16 November**	Malachi 4	John 4.5–26
Saturday	**17 November**	Micah 6.6–8	Colossians 3.12–17
	18 November – 2 before Advent		
Monday	**19 November**	Micah 7.1–7	Matthew 10.24–39
Tuesday	**20 November**	Habakkuk 3.1–19*a*	1 Corinthians 4.9–16
Wednesday	**21 November**	Zechariah 8.1–13	Mark 13.3–8
Thursday	**22 November**	Zechariah 10.6–end	1 Peter 5.1–11
Friday	**23 November**	Micah 4.1–5	Luke 9.28–36
Saturday	**24 November**	*At Evening Prayer the readings for the Eve of Christ the King are used. At other services, the following readings are used:* Exodus 16.1–21	John 6.3–15
	25 November – Christ the King (Sunday next before Advent)		
Monday	**26 November**	Jeremiah 30.1–3, 10–17	Romans 12.9–21
Tuesday	**27 November**	Jeremiah 30.18–24	John 10.22–30
Wednesday	**28 November**	Jeremiah 31.1–9	Matthew 15.21–31
Thursday	**29 November**	Jeremiah 31.10–17 *or* 1st EP of Andrew the Apostle	Matthew 16.13–end
Friday	**30 November**	Andrew the Apostle – see p.71	
Saturday	**1 December**	Isaiah 51.17—52.2	Ephesians 5.1–20

¶ *Collects and Post Communions*

All the contemporary language Collects and Post Communions, including the Additional Collects, may be found in *Common Worship: Collects and Post Communions* (Church House Publishing: London, 2004). The Additional Collects are also published separately.

The contemporary language Collects and Post Communions all appear in *Times and Seasons: President's Edition for Holy Communion.* Apart from the Additional Collects, they appear in the other Common Worship volumes as follows:

- ¶ President's edition: all Collects and Post Communions;
- ¶ *Daily Prayer*: all Collects;
- ¶ main volume: Collects and Post Communions for Sundays, Principal Feasts and Holy Days, and Festivals;
- ¶ *Festivals*: Collects and Post Communions for Festivals, Lesser Festivals, Common of the Saints and Special Occasions.

The traditional-language Collects and Post Communions all appear in the president's edition. They appear in other publications as follows:

- ¶ main volume: Collects and Post Communions for Sundays, Principal Feasts and Holy Days, and Festivals;
- ¶ separate booklet: Collects and Post Communions for Lesser Festivals, Common of the Saints and Special Occasions.

¶ *Lectionary for Dedication Festival*

If date not known, observe on the first Sunday in October or Last Sunday after Trinity.

Evening Prayer on the Eve
Psalm 24
2 Chronicles 7.11–16
John 4.19–29

Dedication Festival *Gold or White*

	Principal Service	3rd Service	2nd Service	Psalmody
Year A	I Kings 8.22–30 *or* Revelation 21.9–14 Psalm 122 Hebrews 12.18–24 Matthew 21.12–16	Haggai 2.6–9 Hebrews 10.19–25	Jeremiah 7.1–11 I Corinthians 3.9–17 *HC* Luke 19.1–10	*MP* 48, 150 *EP* 132
Year B	Genesis 28.11–18 *or* Revelation 21.9–14 Psalm 122 I Peter 2.1–10 John 10.22–29	Haggai 2.6–9 Hebrews 10.19–25	Jeremiah 7.1–11 Luke 19.1–10	*MP* 48, 150 *EP* 132
Year C	I Chronicles 29.6–19 Psalm 122 Ephesians 2.19–22 John 2.13–22	Haggai 2.6–9 Hebrews 10.19–25	Jeremiah 7.1–11 Luke 19.1–10	*MP* 48, 150 *EP* 132

The Blessed Virgin Mary

Genesis 3.8–15, 20; Isaiah 7.10–14; Micah 5.1–4
Psalms 45.10–17; 113; 131
Acts 1.12–14; Romans 8.18–30; Galatians 4.4–7
Luke 1.26–38; *or* 1.39–47; John 19.25–27

Martyrs

2 Chronicles 24.17–21; Isaiah 43.1–7; Jeremiah 11.18–20; Wisdom 4.10–15
Psalms 3; 11; 31.1–5; 44.18–24; 126
Romans 8.35–end; 2 Corinthians 4.7–15; 2 Timothy 2.3–7 [8–13]; Hebrews 11.32–end; 1 Peter 4.12–end; Revelation 12.10–12*a*
Matthew 10.16–22; *or* 10.28–39; *or* 16.24–26; John 12.24–26; *or* 15.18–21

Agnes (21 Jan): *also* Revelation 7.13–end
Alban (22 June): *especially* 2 Timothy 2.3–13; John 12.24–26
Alphege (19 Apr): *also* Hebrews 5.1–4
Boniface (5 June): *also* Acts 20.24–28
Charles (30 Jan): *also* Ecclesiasticus 2.12–end; 1 Timothy 6.12–16
Clement (23 Nov): *also* Philippians 3.17—4.3; Matthew 16.13–19
Cyprian (15 Sept): *especially* 1 Peter 4.12–end; *also* Matthew 18.18–22
Edmund (20 Nov): *also* Proverbs 20.28; 21.1–4, 7
Ignatius (17 Oct): *also* Philippians 3.7–12; John 6.52–58
James Hannington (29 Oct): *especially* Matthew 10.28–39
Janani Luwum (17 Feb): *also* Ecclesiasticus 4.20–28; John 12.24–32
John Coleridge Patteson (20 Sept): *especially* 2 Chronicles 24.17–21; *also* Acts 7.55–end
Justin (1 June): *especially* John 15.18–21; *also* 1 Maccabees 2.15–22; 1 Corinthians 1.18–25
Laurence (10 Aug): *also* 2 Corinthians 9.6–10
Lucy (13 Dec): *also* Wisdom 3.1–7; 2 Corinthians 4.6–15
Oswald (5 Aug): *especially* 1 Peter 4.12–end; John 16.29–end
Perpetua, Felicity and comps (7 Mar): *especially* Revelation 12.10–12*a*; *also* Wisdom 3.1–7
Polycarp (23 Feb): *also* Revelation 2.8–11
Thomas Becket (29 Dec *or* 7 Jul): *especially* Matthew 10.28–33; *also* Ecclesiasticus 51.1–8
William Tyndale (6 Oct): *also* Proverbs 8.4–11; 2 Timothy 3.12–end

Teachers of the Faith and Spiritual Writers

I Kings 3.[6–10] 11–14; Proverbs 4.1–9; Wisdom 7.7–10, 15–16; Ecclesiasticus 39.1–10
Psalms 19.7–10; 34.11–17; 37.31–35; 119.89–96; 119.97–104
I Corinthians 1.18–25; *or* 2.1–10; *or* 2.9–end; Ephesians 3.8–12; 2 Timothy 4.1–8; Titus 2.1–8
Matthew 5.13–19; *or* 13.52–end; *or* 23.8–12; Mark 4.1–9; John 16.12–15

Ambrose (7 Dec): *also* Isaiah 41.9*b*–13; Luke 22.24–30
Anselm (21 Apr): *also* Wisdom 9.13–end; Romans 5.8–11
Athanasius (2 May): *also* Ecclesiasticus 4.20–28; *also* Matthew 10.24–27
Augustine of Hippo (28 Aug): *especially* Ecclesiasticus 39.1–10; *also* Romans 13.11–13
Basil and Gregory (2 Jan): *especially* 2 Timothy 4.1–8; Matthew 5.13–19
Bernard (20 Aug): *especially* Revelation 19.5–9
Catherine of Siena (29 Apr): *also* Proverbs 8.1, 6–11; John 17.12–end
Francis de Sales (24 Jan): *also* Proverbs 3.13–18; John 3.17–21
Gregory the Great (3 Sept): *also* I Thessalonians 2.3–8
Gregory of Nyssa and Macrina (19 July): *especially* I Corinthians 2.9–13; *also* Wisdom 9.13–17
Hilary (13 Jan): *also* I John 2.18–25; John 8.25–32
Irenaeus (28 June): *also* 2 Peter 1.16–end
Jeremy Taylor (13 Aug); *also* Titus 2.7–8, 11–14
John Bunyan (30 Aug): *also* Hebrews 12.1–2; Luke 21.21, 34–36
John Chrysostom (13 Sept): *especially* Matthew 5.13–19; *also* Jeremiah 1.4–10
John of the Cross (14 Dec): *especially* I Corinthians 2.1–10; *also* John 14.18–23
Leo (10 Nov): *also* I Peter 5.1–11
Richard Hooker (3 Nov): *especially* John 16.12–15; *also* Ecclesiasticus 44.10–15
Teresa of Avila (15 Oct): *also* Romans 8.22–27
Thomas Aquinas (28 Jan): *especially* Wisdom 7.7–10, 15–16; I Corinthians 2.9–end; John 16.12–15
William Law (10 Apr): *especially* I Corinthians 2.9–end; *also* Matthew 17.1–9

Bishops and Other Pastors

1 Samuel 16.1, 6–13; Isaiah 6.1–8; Jeremiah 1.4–10; Ezekiel 3.16–21; Malachi 2.5–7
Psalms 1; 15; 16.5–end; 96; 110
Acts 20.28–35; 1 Corinthians 4.1–5; 2 Corinthians 4.1–10 [*or* 1–2, 5–7];
or 5.14–20; 1 Peter 5.1–4
Matthew 11.25–end; *or* 24.42–46; John 10.11–16; *or* 15.9–17; *or* 21.15–17

Augustine of Canterbury (26 May): *also* 1 Thessalonians 2.2*b*–8; Matthew 13.31–33
Charles Simeon (13 Nov): *especially* Malachi 2.5–7; *also* Colossians 1.3–8; Luke 8.4–8
David (1 Mar): *also* 2 Samuel 23.1–4; Psalm 89.19–22, 24
Dunstan (19 May): *especially* Matthew 24.42–46; *also* Exodus 31.1–5
Edward King (8 Mar): *also* Hebrews 13.1–8
George Herbert (27 Feb): *especially* Malachi 2.5–7; Matthew 11.25–end;
also Revelation 19.5–9
Hugh (17 Nov); *also* 1 Timothy 6.11–16
John Keble (14 July): *also* Lamentations 3.19–26; Matthew 5.1–8
John and Charles Wesley (24 May): *also* Ephesians 5.15–20
Lancelot Andrewes (25 Sept): *especially* Isaiah 6.1–8
Martin of Tours (11 Nov): *also* 1 Thessalonians 5.1–11; Matthew 25.34–40
Nicholas (6 Dec): *also* Isaiah 61.1–3; 1 Timothy 6.6–11; Mark 10.13–16
Richard (16 June): *also* John 21.15–19
Swithun (15 July): *also* James 5.7–11, 13–18
Thomas Ken (8 June): *especially* 2 Corinthians 4.1–10 [*or* 1–2, 5–7]; Matthew 24.42–46
Wulfstan (19 Jan): *especially* Matthew 24.42–46

Members of Religious Communities

1 Kings 19.9–18; Proverbs 10.27–end; Song of Solomon 8.6–7; Isaiah 61.10—62.5; Hosea 2.14–15, 19–20
Psalms 34.1–8; 112.1–9; 119.57–64; 123; 131
Acts 4.32–35; 2 Corinthians 10.17—11.2; Philippians 3.7–14; 1 John 2.15–17; Revelation 19.1, 5–9
Matthew 11.25–end; *or* 19.3–12; *or* 19.23–end; Luke 9.57–end; *or* 12.32–37

Aelred (12 Jan): *also* Ecclesiasticus 15.1–6
Alcuin (20 May): *also* Colossians 3.12–16; John 4.19–24
Antony (17 Jan): *especially* Philippians 3.7–14, *also* Matthew 19.16–26
Bede (25 May): *also* Ecclesiasticus 39.1–10
Benedict (11 July): *also* 1 Corinthians 3.10–11; Luke 18.18–22
Clare (11 Aug): *especially* Song of Solomon 8.6–7
Dominic (8 Aug): *also* Ecclesiasticus 39.1–10
Etheldreda (23 June): *also* Matthew 25.1–13
Francis of Assisi (4 Oct): *also* Galatians 6.14–end; Luke 12.22–34
Hilda (19 Nov): *especially* Isaiah 61.10—62.5
Hildegard (17 Sept): *also* 1 Corinthians 2.9–13; Luke 10.21–24
Julian of Norwich (8 May): *also* 1 Corinthians 13.8–end; Matthew 5.13–16
Vincent de Paul (27 Sept): *also* 1 Corinthians 1.25–end; Matthew 25.34–40

Missionaries

Isaiah 52.7–10; *or* 61.1–3*a*; Ezekiel 34.11–16; Jonah 3.1–5
Psalms 67; *or* 87; *or* 97; *or* 100; *or* 117
Acts 2.14, 22–36; *or* 13.46–49; *or* 16.6–10; *or* 26.19–23; Romans 15.17–21; 2 Corinthians 5.11—6.2
Matthew 9.35–end; *or* 28.16–end; Mark 16.15–20; Luke 5.1–11; *or* 10.1–9

Aidan (31 Aug): *also* 1 Corinthians 9.16–19
Anskar (3 Feb): *especially* Isaiah 52.7–10; *also* Romans 10.11–15
Chad (2 Mar *or* 26 Oct): *also* 1 Timothy 6.11*b*–16
Columba (9 June): *also* Titus 2.11–end
Cuthbert (20 Mar *or* 4 Sept): *especially* Ezekiel 34.11–16; *also* Matthew 18.12–14
Cyril and Methodius (14 Feb): *especially* Isaiah 52.7–10; *also* Romans 10.11–15
Henry Martyn (19 Oct): *especially* Mark 16.15–end; *also* Isaiah 55.6–11
Ninian (16 Sept): *especially* Acts 13.46–49; Mark 16.15–end
Patrick (17 Mar): *also* Psalm 91.1–4, 13–end; Luke 10.1–12, 17–20
Paulinus (10 Oct); *especially* Matthew 28.16–end
Wilfrid (12 Oct): *especially* Luke 5.1–11; *also* 1 Corinthians 1.18–25
Willibrord (7 Nov): *especially* Isaiah 52.7–10; Matthew 28.16–end

Any Saint

General

Genesis 12.1–4; Proverbs 8.1–11; Micah 6.6–8; Ecclesiasticus 2.7–13 [14–end]
Psalms 32; 33.1–5; 119.1–8; 139.1–4 [5–12]; 145.8–14
Ephesians 3.14–19; *or* 6.11–18; Hebrews 13.7–8, 15–16; James 2.14–17;
I John 4.7–16; Revelation 21.[1–4] 5–7
Matthew 19.16–21; *or* 25.1–13; *or* 25.14–30; John 15.1–8; *or* 17.20–end

Christian rulers

I Samuel 16.1–13*a*; I Kings 3.3–14
Psalms 72.1–7; 99
I Timothy 2.1–6
Mark 10.42–45; Luke 14.27–33

Alfred the Great (26 Oct): *also* 2 Samuel 23.1–5; John 18.33–37
Edward the Confessor (13 Oct): *also* 2 Samuel 23.1–5; I John 4.13–16
Margaret of Scotland (16 Nov): *also* Proverbs 31.10–12, 20, 26–end;
I Corinthians 12.13—13.3; Matthew 25.34–end

Those working for the poor and underprivileged

Isaiah 58.6–11
Psalms 82; 146.5–10
Hebrews 13.1–3; I John 3.14–18
Matthew 5.1–12; *or* 25.31–end

Elizabeth of Hungary (18 Nov): *especially* Matthew 25.31–end; *also* Proverbs 31.10–end
Josephine Butler (30 May): *especially* Isaiah 58.6–11; *also* I John 3.18–23; Matthew 9.10–13
William Wilberforce, Olaudah Equiano and Thomas Clarkson (30 July): *also* Job 31.16–23;
Galatians 3.26–end, 4.6–7; Luke 4.16–21

Men and women of learning

Proverbs 8.22–31; Ecclesiasticus 44.1–15
Psalms 36.5–10; 49.1–4
Philippians 4.7–8
Matthew 13.44–46, 52; John 7.14–18

Those whose holiness was revealed in marriage and family life

Proverbs 31.10–13, 19–20, 30–end; Tobit 8.4–7
Psalms 127; 128
I Peter 3.1–9
Mark 3.31–end; Luke 10.38–end

Mary Sumner (9 Aug): *also* Hebrews 13.1–5
Monica (27 Aug): *also* Ecclesiasticus 26.1–3, 13–16

The Guidance of the Holy Spirit

Proverbs 24.3–7; Isaiah 30.15–21; Wisdom 9.13–17
Psalms 25.1–9; 104.26–33; 143.8–10
Acts 15.23–29; Romans 8:22–27; 1 Corinthians 12.4–13
Luke 14.27–33; John 14.23–26; *or* 16.13–15

Rogation Days

(7–9 May in 2018)

Deuteronomy 8.1–10; 1 Kings 8.35–40; Job 28.1–11
Psalms 104.21–30; 107.1–9; 121
Philippians 4.4–7; 2 Thessalonians 3.6–13; 1 John 5.12–15
Matthew 6.1–15; Mark 11.22–24; Luke 11.5–13

Harvest Thanksgiving

Year A	**Year B**	**Year C**
Deuteronomy 8.7–18 *or* 28.1–14	Joel 2.21–27	Deuteronomy 26.1–11
Psalm 65	Psalm 126	Psalm 100
2 Corinthians 9.6–end	1 Timothy 2.1–7 *or* 6.6–10	Philippians 4.4–9
Luke 12.16–30 *or* 17.11–19	Matthew 6.25–33	*or* Revelation 14.14–18
		John 6.25–35

Mission and Evangelism

Isaiah 49.1–6; *or* 52.7–10; Micah 4.1–5
Psalms 2; 46; 67
Acts 17.10–end; 2 Corinthians 5.14—6.2; Ephesians 2.13–end
Matthew 5.13–16; *or* 28.16–end; John 17.20–end

The Unity of the Church

Jeremiah 33.6–9*a*; Ezekiel 36.23–28; Zephaniah 3.16–end
Psalms 100; 122; 133
Ephesians 4.1–6; Colossians 3.9–17; 1 John 4.9–15
Matthew 18.19–22; John 11.45–52; *or* 17.11*b*–23

The Peace of the World

Isaiah 9.1–6; *or* 57.15–19; Micah 4.1–5
Psalms 40.14–17; 72.1–7; 85.8–13
Philippians 4.6–9; 1 Timothy 2.1–6; James 3.13–18
Matthew 5.43–end; John 14.23–29; *or* 15.9–17

Social Justice and Responsibility

Isaiah 32.15–end; Amos 5.21–24; *or* 8.4–7; Acts 5.1–11
Psalms 31.21–24; 85.1–7; 146.5–10
Colossians 3.12–15; James 2.1–4
Matthew 5.1–12; *or* 25.31–end; Luke 16.19–end

Ministry, including Ember Days

(See page 7)

Numbers 11.16–17, 24–29; *or* 27.15–end; 1 Samuel 16.1–13*a*; Isaiah 6.1–8; *or* 61.1–3; Jeremiah 1.4–10
Psalms 40.8–13; 84.8–12; 89.19–25; 101.1–5, 7; 122
Acts 20.28–35; 1 Corinthians 3.3–11; Ephesians 4.4–16; Philippians 3.7–14
Luke 4.16–21 *or* 12.35–43 *or* 22.24–27; John 4.31–38 *or* 15.5–17

In Time of Trouble

Genesis 9.8–17; Job 1.13–end; Isaiah 38.6–11
Psalms 86.1–7; 107.4–15; 142.1–7
Romans 3.21–26; Romans 8.18–25; 2 Corinthians 8.1–5, 9
Mark 4.35–end; Luke 12.1–7; John 16.31–end

For the Sovereign

Joshua 1.1–9; Proverbs 8.1–16
Psalms 20; 101; 121
Romans 13.1–10; Revelation 21.22—22.4
Matthew 22.16–22; Luke 22.24–30

The anniversary of HM The Queen's accession is 6 February.

¶ *Psalms in the Course of a Month*

The following provision may be used for a monthly cycle of psalmody in place of the psalms provided in the tables in this booklet. It is based on the provision in The Book of Common Prayer.

	Morning Prayer	**Evening Prayer**
1	1—5	6—8
2	9—11	12—14
3	15—17	18
4	19—21	22—23
5	24—26	27—29
6	30—31	32—34
7	35—36	37
8	38—40	41—43
9	44—46	47—49
10	50—52	53—55
11	56—58	59—61
12	62—64	65—67
13	68	69—70
14	71—72	73—74
15	75—77	78
16	79—81	82—85
17	86—88	89
18	90—92	93—94
19	95—97	98—101
20	102—103	104
21	105	106
22	107	108—109
23	110—112	113—115
24	116—118	119.1–32
25	119.33–72	119.73–96
26	119.97–144	119.145–176
27	120—125	126—131
28	132—135	136—138
29	139—140	141—143
30	144—146	147—150

In February the psalms are read only to the 28th or 29th day of the month.

In January, March, May, July, August, October and December, all of which have 31 days, the same psalms are read on the last day of the month (being an ordinary weekday) which were read the day before, or else the psalms of the monthly course omitted on one of the Sundays in that month.